Body
Mind
and Sugar

E. M. Abrahamson, M.D.
and A. W. Pezet

New York : Henry Holt and Company

PUBLISHED, OCTOBER, 1951
SECOND PRINTING, NOVEMBER, 1952
THIRD PRINTING, JUNE, 1953
FOURTH PRINTING, OCTOBER, 1953
FIFTH PRINTING, MARCH, 1954
SIXTH PRINTING, AUGUST, 1954
SEVENTH PRINTING, FEBRUARY, 1955
EIGHTH PRINTING, AUGUST, 1955
NINTH PRINTING, AUGUST, 1956

80044-0111

Printed in the United States of America.

To

Doctor Seale Harris

Contents

Figures

Body, Mind, and Sugar

Introduction

MEDICAL SCIENCE has made great progress in the twentieth century. Despite its advances, however, the mysteries still outnumber the certitudes. The number of medical papers that begin, "We do not know what," "We do not know why," and "We do not know how," is still formidable. Medical men do not like to admit this to laymen. They have invented words and phrases—neurosis, neurasthenia, and psychoneurosis with depression—to hide their ignorance from the layman and from themselves.

Are the hundreds of thousands, perhaps millions, of people thus labeled suffering from mental or from physical disease? The vast majority of them wander from general practitioner to specialist to psychiatrist without ever finding a cure for the ailments that make their lives a misery to themselves and an irritation to those close to them.

Almost daily one reads of a hitherto considered sane person who has run amuck and killed someone. Even more common are reports of persons who have committed suicide for no reason other than "depression." There are approximately eight thousand murders and twice that number of suicides in the United States every year. Not all of the murders are gang murders, premeditated killings, or accidents. Recently, for example, it was pointed out that of a hundred indicted murderers defended by Judge Samuel Liebowitz in his days as a defense attorney not one had a criminal record. They were people who had killed "in a moment of insanity." And the list of persons who have recently killed themselves while suffering from a "psychoneurosis with depression" reads like a page torn from *Who's Who*.

Since physicians are required to report only communicable diseases, statistics on those suffering from such afflictions as hay fever, asthma, rheumatic fever, and peptic ulcer are not available. The number suffering from the various allergies grouped under hay fever must be enormous. It is large enough for a daily pollen count to be taken throughout North America during the hay fever season, and for newspapers to publish the results. Everyone knows that hay fever and asthma are in some way related, that hay fever sufferers often become asthmatics as they grow older, and that asthmatics get worse and die. In the normal sense, however, asthma is not a fatal disease, but rather one that lingers until death. For rheumatic fever the direct death rate is low, 0.8 per 100,000 for the year 1946 (the latest for which complete statistics are available), but the rate from heart ailments that result from chronic rheumatic fever is twenty times higher. Stomach ulcers, as they are popularly called, cause as many deaths a year as murder. Cancer of the digestive organs is one of the half-dozen greatest causes of death; the number of malignant tumors located in the insulin-secreting islets of the pancreas is only a small fraction of this total.

In the United States there are approximately four million men and women who could be classed as alcoholics. They cannot drink as normal people do. Their drinking is compulsive. In advanced cases, once they start drinking they cannot stop until the alcohol supply is expended or until they finally pass out. What is it that sets these persons apart from their normal fellows?

Doctors and employers alike are becoming aware of the

increasingly large number of people who suffer from chronic fatigue. These people are too tired or too apathetic to do their work, whether occupational or household duties, with satisfactory efficiency.

Pick up a newspaper and you will read of the brilliant pitcher who had a near no-hitter going until the seventh or eighth inning and then "blew up." You will read also of the railroad engineer with the impeccable record of many years who drove past the red signal and wrecked his train.

Why are the greatest number of industrial accidents bunched between mid and late afternoon?

Is there any mental or physical basis for the moral breakdown that underlies all delinquency and crime?

Now these diseases and conditions and happenings and questions appear utterly unrelated. It is the purpose of this book to show you their very close relationship indeed, the result of recent discoveries of their common conditioning.

These discoveries have been made in the laboratory and by means of the scientific method. They have been verified by other workers and recognized in at least one instance by honoring the discoverer with one of the highest awards in the medical field. But the almost obvious implications of these discoveries are still a matter of controversy and not as yet accepted by the medical profession as a whole, largely because most doctors have not as yet had time to read the literature.

Indeed, not all of those whose brilliant thinking and patient labors have contributed to these determinations are aware of the work of others in the same field. In several cases it was the lay member of this collaboration who revealed the existence of parallel work to isolated researchers.

This is not surprising. Scientists often attack similar research projects from vastly different directions. Their work frequently is published in journals devoted to a different speciality. And today the literature in any scientific field is so vast that no man busy working in it, especially the physician with his private and clinical practice, can possibly assimilate it all.

It is also a normal part of what sociologists call "the cultural lag" that new knowledge is slow to influence the behavior of even the minority who can "think." Today, however, we are living at a rate of change so rapid that our very survival may depend upon the speed with which we are able to take advantage of new knowledge. No apology is needed, then, for a book that attempts to disseminate such knowledge.

The subject matter of this book should be the personal concern of more than ten million people at the very least. It is quite possible that their number may be as great as thirty million, one fifth of our population. We have no idea how many persons may be affected in other countries.

Moreover, the factor that brings all these remote and unlikely things together in one category of conditioning, if not of causation, may be the golden key that will in time unlock the closed doors of many other mysteries.

A few years ago Behaviorism was the fashion. Man was an animal and nothing more. His mental processes were but functions of a brain conditioned by external physical stimuli. Now the pendulum has swung to the opposite extreme. Physicians write articles with such titles as "Your Mind Can Control Your Body." The word *psychosomatic,* in which the psychic is placed before the physical only for reasons of euphony, is misinterpreted to give the psychic precedence over the physical.

When doctors and laymen have fully digested the discoveries of the last quarter century to which we call attention in this book, we believe they will agree that all arguments about which is cause and which effect—the body or the mind —are as groundless as the age-old problem of the chicken or the egg. Body and mind are inseparably interrelated. The

[4]

mechanism of their relationship is to be found in the nervous system and the ductless glands.

This book is about the extraordinary part that blood sugar plays in the mechanism that keeps body and mind in healthy balance.

About ourselves: the medical half of our collaboration, E. M. Abrahamson, received his doctorate in chemistry in 1922, and in medicine in 1926. Author of *Office Clinical Chemistry* (Oxford University Press, 1945), he has contributed more than a score of papers to medical and chemical journals. He also is the designer of several pieces of laboratory apparatus now used in the fields of clinical medicine and chemistry. A specialist in diabetes for many years, he has devoted much of his efforts toward clinical research and treatment in hyperinsulinism.

The lay member of our collaboration, A. W. Pezet, was trained at the Massachusetts Institute of Technology and at Harvard University, and is a professional writer of both fiction and nonfiction. In the latter field he has specialized in writing on medical and other scientific subjects for the layman.

This book was conceived through a doctor-patient relationship—Abrahamson having diagnosed Pezet and his wife as being victims of hyperinsulinism. The lay member of our collaboration experienced more than clinical interest in this diagnosis and in the ensuing treatment. Why had he wandered through countless consultations and diagnoses and treatments for more than a decade without relief from his curious symptoms? Why was so little known about a disease condition which affected millions? Why had so little information reached the practicing physician? Why?

The "why's" went unanswered; this was not the first time that the field of medicine had procrastinated in making use of its own knowledge.

[5]

The lay member was determined that a knowledge of hyperinsulinism and its ramifications should be made available to the many who were suffering as he and his wife had suffered. The medical member had already written some half-dozen scientific monographs on the subject, published in various medical journals; he had long wanted to present the facts to the layman and to the physician unreached by the technical treatises.

The result: this book. It has been written in language understandable to the layman. It is hoped, however, that those physicians who may read this will be impelled to consult our sources and to investigate further the theses which we present.

E.M.A.
A.W.P.

New York City
July 18, 1951

1

"... But I Cannot Name the Disease"

*There is a sickness
Which puts some of us in distemper, but
I cannot name the disease.*

—THE WINTER'S TALE, Act I, Scene 2,
Camillo

AT ABOUT two o'clock one cold February morning in 1935, I (Dr. Abrahamson) was called to a patient who was undergoing an attack of paroxysmal tachycardia— a sudden disturbance of the heart causing it to beat at an extremely rapid rate.

When I arrived, the young man was gasping for breath and his chest vibrated with the rapid movements of his heart. His pulse was so fast that I was unable to count it. A quick examination failed to disclose any anatomical trouble. I tried the usual procedures that are supposed to halt such attacks— pressing the eyeballs, pinching the back of the neck, and applying pressure over the carotid arteries in the neck—but the seizure continued. I finally had to administer morphine.

Within a few minutes the heart resumed its regular rate and the young man was quite comfortable. I then thoroughly examined his heart and, finding nothing wrong with it, told him that the attack was not serious. Since there was no organic defect in his heart, he would recover completely without any permanent ill effects. I assured him that he would probably never have another attack.

A few nights later he had another attack. Again morphine was required to stop it. Again examination revealed nothing, and again I assured him that he would no longer be bothered. According to what I had studied, I explained, many persons experience one or two such attacks and then are permanently free of them.

But my patient's heart had not read the medical books, and the poor fellow continued to suffer attacks several times a week. Why he remained under my care is beyond me, for I was certainly a prophet without honor. After a few weeks I suggested that he consult a heart specialist. There was a serious risk of addiction from the repeated injections of morphine.

In those days almost any doctor who owned a cardiograph was considered a heart specialist. But I sent my patient to a cardiologist of unquestioned eminence. He examined my patient physically and with the electrocardiograph. He wrote me a letter confirming my diagnosis of "cardiac neurosis." I was greatly pleased that this outstanding specialist had reached the same conclusion as I. Now that I have matured in medicine, however, I have come to realize that I had merely covered my ignorance with a glib phrase. Cardiac neurosis means a nervous condition which manifests itself by affecting the heart. But what, exactly, is a nervous condition? My patient was a "neurotic" (a diagnosis sometimes made by doctors who do not know what is wrong with their patients).

The thing to do then was to send my patient to a psychiatrist. He would find out what made my patient "nervous" and would remove the hidden cause. The "neurosis" would disappear and with it the palpitation. It all sounded fine. My patient went to a psychiatrist.

At that time I was interested in diabetes and was associated with two large diabetes clinics, one of which I headed. Diabetics are treated with injections of insulin to keep the blood sugar level reasonably close to the normal; the dosage is controlled by determining the sugar content of the blood at fairly frequent intervals. I was setting up the apparatus in my laboratory one afternoon when my patient called me. He was suffering a frightful attack and had to leave his office. He was coming to see me and he would remain until I discovered what was wrong with him, once and for all. It was to be my last chance.

When he arrived, I frankly did not know where to begin. He was panting and I could see the rapid pulsations of the blood vessels in his neck. He was furious, and I had to do something to pacify him, if nothing else. I took him into the laboratory and drew a sample of blood, which I analyzed for sugar. The analysis would take about half an hour—enough time, I hoped, to think of *something!*

The normal fasting blood sugar (that is, in the morning before breakfast) lies between 80 and 120 milligrams of sugar per 100 cubic centimeters of blood. During the day, while food is consumed, it rises to about 140 mg. per 100 cc. When I finished the analysis, I was shocked to find that his blood sugar level was only 52 mg. per 100 cc.! I repeated the determination. It checked.

Now at last I knew why he had these attacks. A similar symptom occasionally occurred in my diabetics when their blood sugar levels fell too much as the result of an overdose of insulin. The condition was called insulin shock. Whenever a diabetic suffered such an attack we administered sugar. Hurriedly I mixed some glucose with water and lemon juice and gave it to my patient to drink. His palpitation stopped within five minutes.

My patient told me how well he now felt. He also related his experiences with the psychiatrist. This was the period when unbridled Freudianism was in its heyday. It was

[9]

fashionable to have a complex or two. The libido, which was discussed only in whispers and only in the inner sanctum of the psychiatrist (the term is now freely used even on the radio), was at the bottom of all our troubles. The patient's subconscious was explored and his libido exhumed. The young man was gravely informed that he had a complex—his subconscious had produced these attacks so that he would have an excuse to avoid his wife. My felonious diagnosis—cardiac neurosis—which had been attested to by the cardiologist was now compounded by the psychiatrist.

Now I knew all the answers. My patient had a deficiency in blood sugar. Logically there was but one thing to do: feed him sugar. It had stopped the seizure right before my eyes. And usually his attacks occurred in the small hours of the night long after his last meal, when his sugar reserves were depleted. So I prescribed disks of dextrose. Ordinary hard candy disks are made from cane sugar which must be converted into dextrose (another name for glucose) and levulose by the digestive apparatus before it can be absorbed by the blood. By using dextrose one step would be eliminated.

My patient bought a box of these tablets and went home. He telephoned me from time to time that he still had attacks quite frequently but that they yielded promptly to the tablets. Soon, however, he reported that the attacks were occurring more frequently. Now he bought the dextrose disks by the case. He had to take them several times an hour. He was unable to sleep through the night. Soon he placed a dish of the tablets on his night table before retiring. During the night he would reach over and take one almost without waking. He was eating so much dextrose that he was becoming positively obese.

I could not understand why he was unable to rid himself of the attacks. After all, I was following sound physiological reasoning. His blood sugar dropped, he had an attack. He took some glucose, his blood sugar rose. The attack stopped. But

[10]

that was not the end of the chain. The attacks persisted in repeating themselves.

One day, however, I came across an article by Dr. Seale Harris, professor of medicine at the University of Alabama. I wrote to Dr. Harris telling him of my patient and asking for help in treating him. Dr. Harris kindly sent me some reprints of his work. It was then that I realized how I had mistreated my patient, and that unwittingly I was responsible for his failure to get well.

Sugar taken into the stomach raises the blood sugar. By using glucose (dextrose) the rise in blood sugar is even more rapid because the glucose does not require digestion. It is absorbed through the walls of the stomach directly into the blood stream. The sudden rise in blood sugar stimulates the production of insulin. My patient had *hyperinsulinism.* His insulin tissue was too sensitive and was overgenerous. Instead of making only the amount of insulin needed to handle the amount of sugar just taken into the blood, an excess of insulin was produced, causing another drop in his blood sugar. His symptoms returned and with them a demand for more glucose. The vicious circle! I treated my patient according to Dr. Harris' directives and he soon completely recovered.

It was through this long-suffering patient that I met *hyperinsulinism,* the opposite of *hypoinsulinism,* which is another name for diabetes, the disease I had specialized in for so many years. The golden key had been placed in my hands but I was still far from fully understanding its use. It is necessary to go back in medical history if Dr. Harris' concept and its implications are to be appreciated.

2

The Old: Diabetes –

MAN'S KNOWLEDGE of the diseases that afflict
him has grown slowly and most unevenly. At first a person
just "got sick" as wild animals do. He either recovered or died.
The first doctors were the medicine men who intoned incantations over the patient, danced and made passes over him, or
touched him with amulets and other sacred objects. Prescrib-
ing a witch's brew of herbs came later. No one knew what
had afflicted him or, if he recovered, what had made him well
again.

It was not until after man had developed the art of writing
that he was able to record his observations of the signs and
symptoms of disease. These recorded observations led to
differentiation among conditions of illness, and what had
been simply sickness gradually became specific diseases. It
is probable that most diseases have existed since the earliest
times. Their incidence, however, may have varied in considerable degree, some becoming more prevalent and others
less.

When we speak of a "new" disease as opposed to an "old"
one, we mean a disease the knowledge of which has been dis-

covered only recently, rather than one which has been recognized for some time as a separate entity. It is of interest to note, then, that the "newest" disease—hyperinsulinism—and one of the "oldest"—hypoinsulinism, or diabetes—are not only curiously related in many ways but also exact medical opposites. More than three thousand four hundred years separate our first recorded knowledge of diabetes and that of hyperinsulinism. Between them lies almost the entire history of medicine. The uncertain and faltering march of that record is well illustrated in the story of diabetes. Thus do we set the stage for what is to come.

During the latter decades of the nineteenth century the Egyptologists were busy. In 1872, at Luxor, George Ebers obtained a papyrus written about 1500 B.C., a millennium before the advent of Hippocrates, the Father of Medicine. Known as the Papyrus Ebers,[1] it has been called "one of the most venerable of medical documents." It gives a number of prescriptions for "medicines to drive away the passing of too much urine." Since the "passing of too much urine" is one of the most obvious signs of diabetes, it is assumed that the disease was known to the ancient Egyptians even at that early date.

Seventeen hundred years later—some five hundred years after Hippocrates' descriptions of tuberculosis, plague, lobar pneumonia, and other respiratory diseases—Aretaeus the Cappadocian gave us the first accurate account of diabetes. It was Aretaeus who also described tetanus, epilepsy, the murmur of heart disease, and the chest *râles* of asthma. Very little is known about this truly remarkable man. Probably a native or resident of the hilly country of Asia Minor above the Euphrates valley in the second century, he wrote in Greek, and his work was lost to us until the middle of the sixteenth century when it was translated into Latin. An English translation appeared in the middle of the nineteenth century, but is only in recent years that Aretaeus' outstanding contribution to the earliest knowledge of diseases has been recognized.

Aretaeus not only gave us our first accurate description of diabetes, he also suggested the origin of the name of the disease. "The fluid," he wrote, "uses the patient's body as a ladder to escape downward." The Greek word for ladder is *Diabaiton. Webster's Unabridged Dictionary* derives "diabetes" through the Latin from the Greek word meaning "to stand with legs apart," as in the position of a ladder.

Although Aretaeus knew the signs and symptoms of diabetes, he recognized only the severer forms of the disease and accordingly considered it a rare and fatal malady. In common with all other ancient writers, he had no idea of its cause or proper treatment.

Fourteen centuries more elapsed before the next step forward was made along the road to a true knowledge of the nature of diabetes. While this step appears simple, it took a hardy scientist with a robust nature to make it, and its results were far-reaching. For it was then that Thomas Willis, the most successful physician of the Restoration, described the sweet taste of diabetic urine.[2]

First stimulated by the publication in 1552 of the Latin translation of Aretaeus' work [3] and now greatly augmented by Thomas Willis, investigations of diabetes became a host in the ensuing years. Soon the adjective "mellitus" was added to the name. Derived from the Latin word *mel,* meaning honey, it acknowledged the fact that sweetness had something important to do with this strange disease. But still no one had any inkling *why.*

During the nineteenth century the incidence of diabetes seemed to increase over that of ancient times. More and more cases were observed and studied. The relationship to acidosis and the peculiar death in coma became fairly well known. But now something happened that has occurred so often in

[14]

the march of science. An epochal discovery was made quite by accident.

It was Oskar Minkowski, born in Russia in 1858, who brought the story of diabetes into our own times (he died only twenty years ago). In 1889 Minkowski had an argument with his associate, von Mering, and to settle it they removed the pancreas from a dog to see if the animal could live without it. The dog died. Other dogs on whom Minkowski repeated the experiment also died. And what they died of was identical in every respect to human diabetes. Before dying the dogs passed excessive amounts of urine which contained from 5 to 10 per cent sugar.[4]

Now we were getting somewhere at last. After three thousand years of observing that diabetics passed excessive amounts of urine—a fact which would logically have led to the belief that the disease had something to do with the kidneys—it was accidentally discovered that the cause must lie in the pancreas.

The pancreas is a compound gland from six to eight inches long, somewhat resembling a bunch of grapes. It is what the gourmet enjoys as sweetbread when it is taken from a calf and served *sauté au beurre noir*. The human pancreas lies transversely along the rear wall of the abdomen with its right end or head in contact with the first part of the small intestine and its left end or tail close to the spleen. One function of the pancreas is to secrete the fluids that help digest proteins, fats, and carbohydrates. There are two ducts which carry these pancreatic juices into the intestine. There are, however, other digestive ferments in the intestine, some derived from the stomach and others from the intestine itself. Obviously, the digestive process is not entirely dependent upon these pancreatic juices. Yet Minkowski's dogs had died when the pancreas was removed. Failure to digest food properly, then, could not be the cause of their deaths—or of diabetes.

In 1869 Langerhans, a young medical student, discovered a

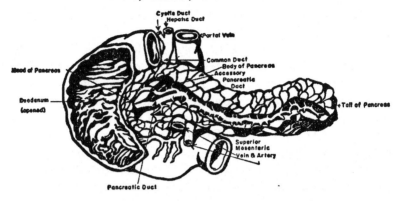

Cystic Duct
Hepatic Duct
Portal Vein
Common Duct
Body of Pancreas
Accessory
Pancreatic
Duct
Head of Pancreas
Duodenum
(opened)
Tail of Pancreas
Superior
Mesenteric
Vein & Artery
Pancreatic Duct

1—Pancreas and Surrounding Structures

The head of the pancreas rests in the curve of the duodenum (the first portion of the bowel). The tail extends toward the left. The superior mesenteric vein, which carries blood from the intestine, and the veins from the pancreas, stomach, and spleen (not shown) empty into the portal vein which carries the blood containing the digestion products and insulin to the liver. The pancreatic duct and the common bile duct together empty into the duodenum; they carry the digestive juice from the pancreas proper and bile from the liver to take part in the digestion of food in the small intestine which is the prolongation of the duodenum. The hepatic duct carries the bile from the liver, while the cystic duct is a side tube connecting the common duct to the gall bladder which stores and concentrates the bile when the opening of the common bile duct and pancreatic duct is closed. When food enters the duodenum, this valve opens, permitting the accumulated secretions to pass into the duodenum.

The islands of Langerhans are scattered throughout the pancreas but are most numerous in the tail. Their secretion does not pass into the pancreatic duct but is picked up by the blood passing through them.

In the illustration the pancreas has been opened to show the duct system.

group of cells in the pancreas [5] that were unconnected and apparently unrelated to the rest of the gland. These *islands of Langerhans have no ducts with which to transmit any secretion.* No one knew what their function was, why they were there.

In 1900, however, Opie performed an autopsy on a girl who had died in diabetic coma. After a careful inspection of all parts of her body, he found the only anatomical abnormality

[16]

to be a degeneration of the islands of Langerhans in the pancreas.[6] Opie found similar cases in which the only apparent abnormality rested in these islands. And so the search narrowed down.

Sixteen years later, Sharpey-Schafer suggested that diabetes was due to a lack of some secretion of the islands of Langerhans. At that time it was already known that there were a number of organs in various parts of the body with typical glandular structure but without ducts with which to carry their secretions elsewhere. These so-called "endocrine," or ductless, glands supply hormones to the body by secreting them into the blood which passes through them. The hormones are used throughout the body. They therefore have no need to be led to a specific place of local and, consequently, limited application. Sharpey-Schafer named the undiscovered hormone from the islands of Langerhans *insulin.*

The search had now become a race. Nearly every laboratory had at least one person making extracts of pancreases obtained from local abattoirs, experimental animals, and autopsy material, in order to obtain the elusive insulin. Everyone knew it was there, but no one was able to get a workable extract.

In 1892, only three years after Minkowski performed the experiment that set us on the right track at last, Frederick Grant Banting was born in Alliston, Ontario. He received his M.D. degree from the University of Toronto the same year that Sharpey-Schafer suggested his hypothetical hormone, insulin. But 1916 was the second year of World War I and Banting enlisted and served with the Canadian army overseas. Mankind, especially the diabetic portion of it, is fortunate that he returned safely to his native land. He settled to the practice of orthopedic surgery in London, Ontario, in 1920. Orthopedics may seem a far cry from diabetes, but Banting was a determined young man with an idea.

He gave up his practice and received permission to use

[17]

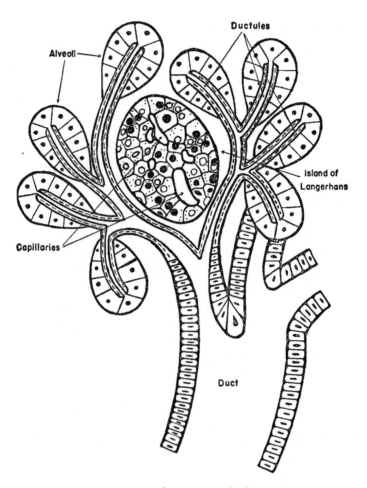

2—*Structure of the Pancreas* (*Schematic*)

The ducts leading from the tiny bulbs (alveoli), whose cells pour their secretion into the central space, join to form progressively larger ducts which finally constitute the two pancreatic ducts. The islands of Langerhans are not connected with this duct system. These cells manufacture insulin which passes through the walls of the cells and of the tiny blood vessels to reach the blood. The blood capillaries join larger ones which finally empty into the pancreatic vein and thence into the portal vein. (An island of Langerhans may be visualized by imagining a loosely skeined length of cord winding around within a bag of peas. The cord will roughly represent the capillaries, the peas

[18]

the laboratory of the University of Toronto to work on his idea. A second-year medical student, Charles H. Best, was assigned to help him.

The idea? Like most great ones it was quite simple, once someone had the imagination to think of it. None of the extracts that had been made so far from pancreatic material was successful because the external secretions of the pancreas —those that did not originate in the islands of Langerhans— being digestants, digested the island tissue and destroyed the very insulin that everyone was seeking. So Banting and Best operated on a dog, tying those ducts leading from the pancreas to the intestine which normally carry the pancreatic digestive juice. The pancreas could not dispose of its secretion, which backed up, producing a degeneration of the pancreatic tissue. But it did not injure the island of Langerhans tissue, since it was a separate organ situated within the pancreas. The experimental dog did not develop diabetes.

After several weeks they removed these degenerated pancreases from this and other experimental dogs and made extracts from them. The extracts were then injected into dogs that had been rendered diabetic by removal of their pancreases. These dogs were kept alive and in good health for long periods of time. They next mixed some of their extract with pancreatic juice. This mixture was without effect on experimental diabetics. We know now that, like meat, insulin is a protein and is digested by the protein-digesting ferments. This is why insulin must be injected. When given by mouth it is digested like any food, thus being destroyed and of no benefit to the diabetic.[7]

Even after Banting's epoch-making experiment, we were still a long way from the commercial preparation of insulin. If we had to make the extract as Banting did, diabetics would

the cells of the island, and the bag the limiting membrane. In the illustration the capillaries may be cut directly across to give a round section, while a slanting cut shows a long oval section.)

still die in coma because there would not be enough insulin to supply the demand. Once the implications of Banting's reasoning were understood, the solution of the problem of preparing insulin from abattoir material was simple. The pancreatic juice contains trypsin which is active only in slightly alkaline solutions. All that was necessary to prepare insulin from any animal pancreas was to inactivate the trypsin with acid. Insulin extracts are made therefore by treating the pancreases with dilute hydrochloric acid. The extract is then purified and concentrated, with the various commercial strengths prepared from these potent solutions.

Until the discovery of insulin the treatment of diabetes had been simple and ineffectual. In view of our present knowledge it is a vivid example of the flounderings of medicine in the pursuit of knowledge.

Methods of chemical analysis had developed so that the physician could follow his case with quantitative measurement. There are three kinds of food: proteins, such as meat, fish, and cheese; carbohydrates, the starchy foods and sweets; and fats. We already knew that carbohydrates and proteins would furnish 4.1 calories per gram and fats 9.3. The caloric requirements of the body were also known. The body requires just so much protein per day. In addition to the energy content of proteins as fuel, they also supply essential elements to repair the wear and tear of living and to build up the tissues of the body. The amount of protein we require and the amount that the appetite will demand are fairly well fixed, so that adjustments of diet must come in the quantity of carbohydrate and fat we eat.

Based upon these facts, the treatment devised for the poor diabetic was to starve him for a few days. Some doctors even went so far as to give him "doughnuts" made of talcum powder fried in mineral oil and sweetened with saccharin. In other words, they let the patient go through the motions of eating without supplying him with any nourishment. This was kept up until his urine was free of sugar. Then he was fed gradually increasing amounts of real food until a trace of sugar appeared in his urine. The food supply was diminished only enough to remove that trace. His physicians now knew his "total carbohydrate tolerance," which was calculated from the protein and fat as well as the carbohydrate in his diet.

In digestion all of the carbohydrates are converted into sugar. Some 56 per cent of the proteins also are converted into sugar, but only 10 per cent of the fats. To prevent starvation the body must receive a certain minimum of calories of food energy. Since protein is not very variable, and since the diabetic can utilize only a limited amount of carbohydrate, energy requirements had to be made up by increasing the intake of fats.

Fats are compounds of glycerin $[C_3H_5(OH)_3]$ and the fatty acids. The latter in combination with alkalies are familiar to us in the form of ordinary soap. Acetic acid is a fatty acid common to our daily experience; vinegar, for example, is a 3 per cent solution of acetic acid. The simplest fatty acid is formic acid (HCOOH), which we encounter whenever an insect stings us. The many fatty acids differ only in the length and complexity of the carbon chain in their make-up. (*Note* I, p. 196.)

Fats are a useful fuel to be burned in supplying energy for our activities. The process of burning is effected by the combination of other elements with oxygen. This may occur slowly as in the gradual formation of oxide of iron (rust) on an unused rail exposed to water or moist air. It occurs more rapidly when we burn coal or oil in a furnace. The combination is sudden and violent in the explosion of gunpowder or dynamite. The process is the same in the controlled explosion of gasoline and air in the internal combustion engine. When fats are burned in the body, the process is a slow, step-by-step combination of carbon and hydrogen atoms with oxygen. These various kinds of burning differ only in their duration. (*Note* II, p. 197.)

The diabetic diets which resulted from increasing the intake of fats were not very palatable. But a far worse objection was soon discovered.

"Fats burn in the flame of carbohydrate, but in its absence they smoke," was the aphorism in vogue a few years ago. Unless glucose—that particular kind of sugar to which the digestive process converts food—is being combusted, the body cannot completely burn fats. The glycerin part of the fat readily converts into glucose and burns. But the remaining fatty acids are incompletely burned, resulting in the production of large amounts of diacetic acid and acetone. These appear in the urine where their presence may be detected by chemical tests. Diacetic acid is quite strong and is poisonous. It breaks down spontaneously to lose carbon dioxide, leaving a residue of acetone. (*Note* III, p. 198.) (Acetone frequently may be found in commercial nail polish removers.) Before diacetic acid and acetone appear in the urine, they first suffuse the blood, where the diacetic acid combines with the alkali in the blood, carrying it to the urine. This depletes the blood of its alkaline reserve. The patient becomes drowsy, then stuporous; if the condition is severe, he goes into a coma and finally dies. This process is called acidosis.

Acetone is extremely volatile, and some of it will be excreted through the patient's lungs. In the days before Banting's discovery, interns in diabetes wards would make their rounds sniffing the breath of patients to detect those who would soon die.

In mild cases of acidosis all of the diacetic acid is converted to acetone. Since acetone is not acidic, its excretion in the urine does not deplete the body of alkalies. But if the urine of an acidotic patient contained diacetic acid in addition to acetone, it was often necessary to inject bicarbonate of soda

[22]

into the veins to restore the alkali reserve. This condition could be detected by direct chemical examination of the blood, as well as by the presence of diacetic acid in the urine.

Prior to the discovery of insulin, then, all diabetic treatment was directed toward staving off the inevitable end as long as possible. In all but the milder forms of the disease the story was always the same. Unless the patient died accidentally or from some other disease, such as pneumonia, eventually he arrived at the comatose ending.

The liver normally contains a considerable amount of glycogen, the animal starch which it manufactures from the glucose coming from the gastrointestinal tract. When we absorb more carbohydrate than we require, the excess, after the liver is saturated with glycogen, is converted into fat and stored in the loose, adipose tissue of the body. In the diabetic the paucity of insulin prevents the liver from storing glycogen. The space is taken up by fat. (The old diabetes wards harbored many patients having large livers with fatty degeneration.) This leads to a failure of the liver to handle fats, and often the blood becomes milky from the large content of fat globules suspended in it. Some of this fatty or waxy material is *cholesterol,* a substance of prime importance to the body. While all its functions are not yet clearly understood, we do know that its presence in the bile enables us to digest fats by emulsifying them. Cholesterol also is related chemically to vitamin D and to the sex and adrenal hormones, and is believed to be a source for their manufacture.

If cholesterol is fed to rabbits [8] the excess will separate out on the walls of the blood vessels and form *atheromatous plaques.* These become filled with calcium salts and the animal then has arteriosclerosis (hardening of the arteries). As yet it has not been completely established that the same mechanism causes human arteriosclerosis. A report has just been published [9] on research done by Dr. John W. Gofman and his associates of the Donner Laboratory of Medical Physics at the University of California. It indicates that high blood cholesterol is not always a precursor of arteriosclerosis. Only when the cholesterol is present in what Dr. Gofman has termed "giant molecules, S-f 10–20" does the dreaded disease result. Long ago, however, it was noticed that when diabetics had an excess of cholesterol in the blood they were extremely prone to the development of arteriosclerosis. "Diabetic gangrene" of the toes was frequently observed in the pre-Banting diabetes wards. It was, of course, due to advanced hardening of the arteries and was really arteriosclerotic gangrene. The same process of the narrowing of the blood vessels led to what was called "diabetic retinitis," which seriously impaired the patient's vision.

The diabetic was prey to other complications of his disease. His blood was so rich in sugar that it was an excellent culture medium for bacteria. Whenever he had an infection it increased the metabolic demand on his body, making his diabetic condition worse.

The bleak prospect of the diabetic has been changed completely by Banting's epochal discovery. When insulin became commercially available, the diabetic's chance to live took a sharp upward swing. In fact, there was now no reason for an uncomplicated case of diabetes ever to be hospitalized. Is it any wonder that Banting's work on his behalf was crowned with the Nobel Prize?

We knew now that diabetes was due to a deficiency of insulin. With that life-saving substance available, the treatment was considered quite simple. In practice it was not, as we were soon to discover. And in thinking it simple we managed to complicate it even more in various erroneous and futile ways. Conditioned by our previous experience, our minds could not shake off the shackles of the past.

The first automobiles were called horseless carriages. All

carriages were equipped with buggy-whip holders. Hence, the first automobiles were equipped with buggy-whip holders. Q.E.D. Such is the stubborn inertia of the human mind. It is not surprising, then, that even after insulin was available and being regularly injected into diabetic patients, we still went through the rigmarole of determining the patient's "carbohydrate tolerance."

We knew that the proportions of carbohydrate and fat should be so regulated that not too much of the latter would be taken. In order to provide enough calories we had to increase the carbohydrate. We knew that 1 unit of insulin would handle 2½ grams of carbohydrate. So we added enough carbohydrate to furnish the required calories and to prevent the incomplete burning of the fat (so that the patient would not go into acidosis), and we covered the carbohydrate in excess of the "tolerance" with insulin at the rate of 1 unit for every 2½ grams. The diet was arranged so that one third of the carbohydrate was consumed at each meal. Efforts were made to keep the insulin intake at a minimum, commensurate with keeping the patient alive and reasonably comfortable.

When it comes to food, however, the diabetic is an incorrigible thief. Interns and nurses would discover him prowling the hospital corridors at night, trying to beg, borrow, or steal food from other patients. He would encourage his well-meaning but unknowing visitors to bring him fruit and even candy. His night table would be searched periodically for the purloined food hidden there.

Despite these handicaps we gravely continued to observe the patient's carbohydrate tolerance. We were so careful! In the hospital's special diet kitchen each dish of food was weighed both before and after the patient's meal, to determine exactly how many grams he had eaten. Even if the diabetic had cooperated fully—had followed his diet, had not stolen food—still, this weighing of the food would have been a meaningless gesture. It is conceivable, for example, that two

[25]

oranges might have approximately the same weight. It is equally conceivable, however, that they might contain completely different amounts of sugar. It was senseless to weigh food whose composition could only be guessed. But we all did it.

In the hospital and clinic the patient's diet would be selected from a number of standard diets. He would receive a printed copy of that diet which was the nearest to his individual needs, depending upon his weight and the amount of physical activity associated with his occupation. (In the office of the diabetes specialist the diabetic could obtain a custom-built diet, designed for himself alone.)

After a few weeks of careful adjustment the patient was presented with his final diet and insulin prescription. He was taught to administer his own insulin injections. (There was even a portable scale on the market, with which the diabetic supposedly weighed his food both at home and when dining out.) He was warned to follow instructions, and sent home.

It was all in vain. Having ceased to be dangerous, the life of the diabetic had now become complicated. Within two or three days all dietary instructions had gone out the window. And frequently the diabetic had to return to the hospital. It was then that the diabetes specialist decided it would be much simpler to prescribe a single standardized diet rather than one of several select diets, since the diabetic invariably would ignore the diet anyway . . . !

The sugar that appears in the urine of diabetics is not really a disease process. The real abnormality in diabetes is the excessive *blood* sugar, while urinary sugar is merely an expression of the body's attempt to correct this abnormality by ridding itself of some of it. If that safety device were not present, the blood sugar would accumulate so excessively that the blood would become too thick to flow through the finer blood vessels. Urinary sugar analysis, therefore, essentially is indicative only of the sugar lost in the urine and consequently only of partial value in diabetic treatment. A casually passed specimen of urine is not of much significance; diabetes specialists use a sample collected over a twenty-four-hour period. By analyzing a part of this sample and then multiplying the percentage of sugar by the total volume, a reasonably reliable estimate is obtained of the total amount of lost sugar in a day. Some amounts are startling. Diabetics have been known to pass more than a pound of sugar in one day.

The term commonly used—1 per cent or 2 per cent sugar—actually is meaningless. A 2 per cent sugar urine will drop to 1 per cent, for example, by the simple expedient of drinking twice as much water. The amount of sugar determining the actual severity of the diabetes remains unchanged. Only when the excretion is expressed in grams can an accurate judgment be made. It is generally considered satisfactory if a diabetic excretes less than 15 grams of sugar per day.

One diabetic, who had been under observation at one of New York City's large diabetes clinics for several years, never excreted more than 10 grams of sugar for any day that he was under study. One day, however, he happened to have symptoms and signs of a kidney stone and was sent to the kidney clinic, where a urine specimen was analyzed. It contained 8 per cent sugar—one hundred times as much as had ever been found in the diabetes clinic over a period of years! The mystery was soon solved. For a day or two before reporting to the diabetes clinic, the patient was conscious of his diabetes and consequently watched his diet. The rest of the time, however—and it was during one of these periods that he was examined at the kidney clinic—he ate essentially what he pleased. Unless, then, reports of diabetes clinics are based upon frequent determinations of the sugar actually in the blood, little reliance can be placed in them. The blood sugar

[27]

cannot be affected by a short period of "cramming" the proper diet.

After a while they stopped putting buggy-whip holders in automobiles. So, too, physicians began to question the need for determining the diabetic's carbohydrate tolerance.

Assume a patient has a tolerance of 100 grams of carbohydrate. At the ratio of 2½ grams of carbohydrate to 1 unit of insulin, the patient's own insulin apparatus is supplying about 40 units of insulin a day. Thus, if we wish to feed him 200 grams of carbohydrate, he will require an additional 40 units of insulin a day. And if we should increase his starch intake to 300 grams, we must give him 80 units of insulin. If we give him so much carbohydrate, however, we must cut down on the fats, since the protein requirements are relatively constant.

Two Viennese doctors, Adlersberg and Porges, conducted just such an experiment.[10] To their pleasant surprise their patients were kept in balance with considerably *less* insulin than they had needed when taking only 100 grams of carbohydrate. A revolutionary discovery had been made: *diabetics are best treated by restricting the fats.* Now the doctors as well as the patients discarded the old diets.

It was difficult, however, to convince the diabetic of the new concept. If sugar appears in the urine we must be taking in too much sugar. We must therefore restrict the intake of carbohydrates, since they are entirely converted into sugar. This was good logic. Logic is that science which deals with the derivation of conclusions from premises according to the laws of valid reasoning. What is seldom recognized is that while the *reasoning* might be valid, invalid *premises* lead logically and inexorably to invalid conclusions. We must re-examine our premises.

Himsworth has shown that diabetics were not excessive eaters of starch before they developed the disease.[11] *They were excessive eaters of fats.* He has shown that the nations

[28]

and peoples whose diet is mostly carbohydrate—such as the Chinese and Japanese, whose staple food is rice—have very little diabetes. On the other hand, the Jews who consume so much animal fat, and the Italians with their large use of olive oil, are most afflicted with the disease.[12]

We know now that fat is definitely depressing to the activity of the insulin apparatus. The secretion of insulin is stimulated by a rise in blood sugar. We therefore actually tend to ameliorate diabetes by withholding fat and furnishing larger amounts of carbohydrate. With such a diet the patients are kept in good health by giving them enough insulin to meet their requirements. A sensible treatment is to give the patient an outline of about what he should eat. The dosage of insulin is slowly increased until the urine is reasonably free from sugar and the blood sugar is at an optimum. We are all creatures of habit. Once we are accustomed to a diet we will follow it with only occasional minor variations, provided that it meets one essential requirement: it must satisfy our palates.

At first insulin was injected before each meal. It had to be. The first insulin to appear on the market was an extract of the pancreases of cattle, and its action began in about twenty minutes and lasted from four to five hours. The diabetic therefore had to take his insulin twenty minutes before each meal, so that the peak of its action occurred while the food was being absorbed. In the course of time the solutions on the market became better refined and more concentrated, so that it became possible to inject the same dose in smaller bulk, lessening the discomfort of the injection. But the diabetic still had to take an injection at least three times a day. Frequently it was necessary to have an extra injection and feeding at bedtime.

Even after we had insulin, diabetics were quite often brought to the hospital in a coma. In such cases the mere administration of insulin was not sufficient to restore consciousness. The *normal* blood sugar—that is, not during the fasting or before-breakfast state—is about 140 milligrams of sugar per 100 cubic centimeters of blood. A severe diabetic might have a blood sugar of 300 mg. in the *fasting* state. This may appear extremely excessive—more than twice the normal —but there are 6,000 cc. of blood in the body. An extra 200 mg. in blood sugar would mean that the blood has 12 grams more sugar than it should. Since 1 unit of insulin will enable the consumption of 2½ grams of glucose (the form sugar takes in the body), only about 5 units of insulin would deplete the diabetic of this 12-gram excess. Since it may take as much as 500 units, or even more, to restore a comatose patient to consciousness, a glucose solution is given intravenously, plus insulin in the ratio of 1 unit to every 2½ grams. In order to be in coma the patient must have been neglectful of his condition for some time, and the injected glucose is avidly absorbed by the liver to restore its depleted stock of glycogen (the substance into which the liver changes glucose for storage).

If the comatose patient has been in acidosis for some time, the leakage of alkali induced by the excretion of diacetic acid lowers the alkali reserve. Sodium bicarbonate necessary to restore that reserve must be injected—either separately or with the glucose. Lactate also may be used for this purpose.

At times (but rarely now), the process of alkali depletion has gone so far that irreversible changes have taken place and the patient cannot be roused from his coma. He sinks into death despite the most heroic efforts to save him. If we could get diabe*tics* under control, deaths in coma would practically disappear. Much will be said later, in another connection, of the diabetic's sanguine, happy-go-lucky temperament that makes him prone to neglect those things he must do to save his own life.

An excess of cholesterol in the blood—one of the dangerous by-product complications of diabetes and an indication of the liver's impairment in its function of handling fats—can now be controlled by judicious use of "lipotropic substances" which improve the liver's ability to metabolize fats. Thus the terrors of diabetes largely have been removed.

In the years immediately following the discovery of insulin, many efforts were made to prolong its action so that it would no longer be necessary for the patient to take the minimum three injections a day. Attempts also were made to prepare insulin by chemical synthesis, so that we would not be dependent upon animal sources for our supply. In addition, a synthetic product is uniform and becomes less expensive than the natural product as production methods are improved. The synthetic production of adrenalin already had been accomplished. Why should it not be possible to do the same with its fellow hormone, insulin?

The first step in the artificial manufacture of any organic substance is its purification for purposes of accurate quantitative analysis, so that we may know not only its exact chemical composition but also its chemical structure. In order to purify any substance we first must crystallize it. The snowflake and the diamond are examples of the purity of the crystalline forms of water and carbon, respectively.

In 1926 Abel succeeded in preparing insulin crystals.[13] But neither he nor anyone else so far has been able to prepare insulin crystals free from zinc, or one of several other metals. (There is more zinc in the pancreas than in any other organ of the body.) Abel's crystalline insulin, which has a potency of 22 units per mg., has been adopted as the international standard. But all efforts to analyze it completely so far have failed. We do know that it is of protein nature, and of so complicated a structure that it is doubtful if it ever will be made chemically.

In 1936, however, H. C. Hagedorn succeeded in producing a form of insulin with a more prolonged action than either ordinary or crystalline insulin. He combined the crystalline insulin with *protamine* derived from the sperm of the rainbow trout. Protamines are a kind of protein that can precipitate

[31]

other proteins from solution. His product, Protamine-Zinc-Insulin (universally known as P.Z.I.), was a notable advance.[14] Solutions of ordinary and of crystalline insulin are both somewhat acid. When they are used, the tissue juices pour into the area of injection to neutralize the irritating acid fluid. The insulin is picked up and carried by the blood to wherever it is needed. By adjusting the P.Z.I. solution so that it resembles the blood in being slightly alkaline, the precipitated compound of insulin acts as a depot whence insulin is liberated slowly. Instead of occurring in about twenty minutes, as with ordinary and crystalline insulin, the peak of its action occurs as long as twenty-four hours after the injection and its effects are noticeable for some ninety-six hours. By using P.Z.I. the patient could get along with only one injection a day. Hagedorn realized, of course, that his P.Z.I. could not be used in the treatment of coma where a quick response was essential, but he felt it would be excellent for maintaining the good health of the diabetic.

These hopes, however, were not entirely fulfilled. Despite the acclaim that P.Z.I. received, it was only another step forward and not the final answer. We sleep during the night and consume food during less than half of each twenty-four hours. It was soon realized that diabetics require their insulin during the early part of the day and not during the night's rest. If the single injection of P.Z.I. were to replace the three or four injections of ordinary insulin effectively, something would have to be done about this time factor. In attempting to solve the problem other substances were combined with insulin. Globin insulin,[15] histone insulin,[16] and many other combinations were tried, and some even reached the market. These had time-activity periods intermediate between that of regular and protamine-zinc-insulin. Patients were then treated with two injections in the morning—a small dose of regular insulin to control breakfast and a larger dose of P.Z.I. to take care of the rest of the twenty-four hours. This gave the patient

[32]

two needle pricks a day instead of three or four, but by taking them both at the same time, he at least was spared the discomfort and embarrassment of having to carry a hypodermic syringe.

Soon it was found that the two kinds of insulin could be combined in the same syringe. Since P.Z.I. contains more than enough protamine to combine with all the insulin in it, the mixture had to be made with sufficient insulin to combine with the excess protamine and still leave free insulin to achieve the immediate effect desired.[17] The amount of insulin added to the P.Z.I. depended upon the experience of the individual doctor. Three-to-one and two-to-one mixtures were the most popular. Whatever the ratio, they were made by simply taking up the two solutions in the same syringe and shaking them together before injection. This treatment has now been in use for several years. A possibly objectionable feature is the necessity of using two bottles of insulin, thus permitting errors in dosage.

After a lengthy period of development, N.P.H. Insulin was placed on the market in September, 1950.[18] Its unabbreviated name is Neutral Protamine Hagedorn Insulin, named for Hagedorn, who has had most to do with its development and in whose laboratory it was first prepared. It is a suspension of tiny crystals and thus a pure substance of definite construction. N.P.H. Insulin has its most pronounced action during the first twelve hours, after which its effects taper off for another twenty-four hours. If administered daily before breakfast, therefore, there is sufficient overlap to provide insulin at all times, while the major part of the substance's activity is concentrated at that time of day at which it is most needed.

All physicians with experience in treating diabetics realize that each patient is a law unto himself. While N.P.H. insulin is effective in most cases, it does not always work. A few patients become ravenously hungry in the afternoon (indicating a fall in blood sugar) and then spill large amounts of sugar in the morning urine. It is futile to try to change their eating habits by shifting the timing of their meals—the patients simply will not cooperate. In such cases, we must use one of the other forms of insulin, such as globin insulin or the mixtures described above or, perhaps, multiple doses of unmodified insulin. With a little patience and ingenuity, each patient can be controlled with that form of the hormone which proves best for him.

Further progress in understanding diabetes can be expected. There can be no doubt, for example, that the islands of Langerhans are not alone in producing diabetes. A century ago the great Claude Bernard performed an experiment on a number of animals. He called it *piqûre diabétique*.[19] He punctured the floor of the first ventricle (a space within the brain) and the animal's blood sugar rose, with the excess pouring into the urine. This condition, however, was only temporary, and complete recovery followed.

Houssay removed the pituitary gland from dogs. After they had recovered from the operation, he removed the pancreas. In spite of having no pancreas, the Houssay dogs did not develop diabetes. But when anterior pituitary extract was administered they became diabetic. And by injecting very large amounts of anterior pituitary extract into normal dogs, they too manifested the increased blood sugar and the urinary sugar discharge of diabetes.[20]

Charles H. Best, who as a student had assisted Banting, administered large amounts of insulin together with tested pituitary extracts that were known to have been effective in producing diabetes in unprotected animals. These insulin-protected dogs did not develop the signs of diabetes.[21] Thus, the pituitary, which has been called "the master gland of the body," must have some definite relation to diabetes.

When phlorizin is administered to animals, or even to man, sugar appears in the urine without any rise in blood sugar.[22] This condition must result from an effect on the kidneys, and it subsides after withdrawal of the drug. During the past few years a number of researchers have injected alloxan, a substance related chemically to uric acid, into animals.[23] These animals developed a disease indistinguishable from diabetes, and post-mortem examinations revealed visible evidence of injury to the islands of Langerhans.

What all this may lead to, only further research can tell. We do not as yet know the precise details of the action of insulin in the body. An inkling of one phase of this action is somewhat analogous to that of a candle. If we set a match to wax, it will not burn. But if the wax has a wick, we can obtain light from it, and the wick is consumed along with the wax. This is somewhat similar to the action of insulin with glucose. Glucose is needed to furnish energy to every cell in the body. It is the fuel of the body. Each time you move an arm, your muscles burn glucose. You also burn glucose in your brain when you think! Insulin is the wick that makes such combustion possible. It is essential to the thought and movement which distinguish living matter from inanimate matter.

Insulin has another action. The body is so constituted that it can function satisfactorily under fairly circumscribed conditions. For example, the normal temperature of our bodies is 98.6° Fahrenheit. This "normal," however, is the median of a slight up-and-down variation. Thus, when we arise our temperature is about 98.0° F., while for about half an hour after each meal it is 99.0° F. If it rises to 100.0° F., we have fever and are sick. If it falls to 97.5° F. we have a chill and are sick. Under hot conditions we perspire and the evaporation of the water on our skin cools us off and keeps our temperature normal. If we are exposed to cold, we shiver and the automatic muscular work done raises the body's temperature to normal.

The blood sugar level is also important for the efficient operation of the body. Like the body's temperature, blood

[35]

sugar level fluctuates about a "normal range." Whenever it goes above or below that range, we are sick. The normal blood sugar level supposedly is 80–120 mg. per 100 cc. of blood. This is not strictly true, however, for that is the normal *fasting* blood sugar level—the level before breakfast, or long after our last evening meal. But fasting is not a normal state. We are not comfortable. We are hungry. Hence, the normal blood sugar level during the active periods of the day is about 140 on the same scale. This is similar to the difference in temperature between the 98.0° on arising and 98.6° during the day's activity.

The total amount of sugar in the entire blood stream is less than two teaspoonfuls. When we eat a meal the products of the digestion of that meal are taken up by the blood. If they were taken directly into the general circulation, a single two-ounce potato would flood the blood with many times as much sugar as it normally contains. The blood that leaves the stomach and the intestines, however, carries their products of digestion to the liver. Similarly, the blood leaving the islands of Langerhans does not go directly into the general circulation but first to the liver. There, under the influence of insulin brought to it from the islands of Langerhans, the glucose (animal sugar) from the products of digestion is converted into glycogen (animal starch). Like ordinary sugar, glucose is soluble in water, but glycogen is not, thus enabling the liver to hold the material within it. If this conversion did not take place the sugar would be washed right through the liver into the general circulation.

The blood that leaves the liver contains the proper amount of sugar. It also carries that portion of the insulin which was not required to convert glucose into glycogen. This excess insulin circulates with the blood throughout the body, enabling each cell to utilize the glucose. It is the wick in the candle.

Let us consider the chain of events that occur when we eat some carbohydrate. It is digested and converted to glucose,

[36]

which passes from the gastrointestinal tract into the blood. This blood goes through the liver via the portal vein. There being no insulin in this blood, the sugar passes unchanged through the liver into the general circulation, thus increasing the blood sugar level. When the enriched blood now reaches the pancreas, the *rise* in blood sugar stimulates the insulin machinery to work. Insulin is secreted by the islands of Langerhans into the blood and is carried through the portal vein back to the liver. There the subsequent sugar-rich portions of blood from the stomach and intestines have the greater part of their glucose filtered out and stored as glycogen. The blood now leaving the liver contains the proper amount of sugar.

A dam is a barrier between two levels of water. Nothing occurs as the higher water level fluctuates unless it reaches the top of the dam. The excess water then spills over. Similarly, if the blood sugar level exceeds its normal—about 140 mg. per 100 cc. of blood—and reaches about 165, it spills over into the urine. This action occurs if the kidneys are normal. Sometimes, however, the kidneys' "renal threshold" is low, and sugar will appear in the urine despite normal levels in the blood. This condition, known as *renal diabetes*, is quite harmless. On the other hand, severely damaged kidneys may fail to pass any sugar, in spite of very high levels in the blood. Persons with that combination have diabetes without ever actually showing any trace of sugar in the urine. Sugar in the urine, then, merely represents an economic waste. It is the result of a compensatory attempt by the kidneys to correct an unnatural situation—overrich blood.

In the vast majority of cases in which diabetes is suspected, the suspicion can be confirmed or denied by a simple test of the urine passed about two hours after a meal. If the meal has included considerable amounts of starchy foods, the presence or absence of sugar in the specimen will be highly indicative of the existence or absence of diabetes.

[37]

If the specimen contains but a small amount of sugar, the case may be *renal diabetes.* This is the entirely harmless condition in which the level at which sugar filters into the urine is abnormally low. If, on the other hand, the specimen is sugar free and the patient nevertheless has such usual symptoms of diabetes as excessive urine and thirst because of the great loss of water, then the condition may be *diabetes insipidus.* This entirely different illness is due to disease of the pituitary gland within the brain. Another condition sometimes occurs in women toward the end of pregnancy, or during the nursing period, in which they excrete lactose (milk sugar). Again, there is a perfectly innocuous condition called *pentosuria,* wherein sugars called "pentoses" (containing five carbon atoms instead of the six of glucose) are found in the urine. Occasionally this will occur in otherwise normal people who have eaten such fruits as apples and plums which contain significant amounts of pentoses. Pentosuria is without significance insofar as an individual's health is concerned.

In all cases in which there is the slightest doubt, the Glucose Tolerance Test will give the doctor the right answer. There are several modifications of this test in vogue. The simplest and the one used most extensively consists in taking a sample of the blood in the fasting state, before breakfast. The patient then drinks 100 grams of glucose dissolved in water, flavored with lemon juice. Blood and urine samples are taken at half-hour intervals for two hours. The results are plotted on a graph similar to the one on the next page.

In the case of a healthy person, all the urine specimens should be sugar free. The initial blood sugar level should lie between 80 and 120 mg. per 100 cc. of blood. The level should rise to not more than 160 in thirty or sixty minutes, and it should return to its initial value within two hours. If these conditions are not met, the patient has diabetes. The severity of his case may be judged to some extent by the height to which the blood sugar level rises.

[38]

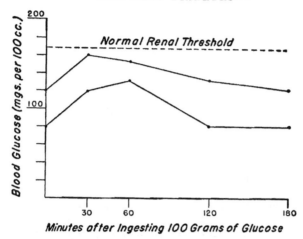

3—The Glucose Tolerance Test

The upper solid line denotes the maximum normal blood sugar values after the patient has drunk the 100-gram glucose solution. Any result above this line would indicate diabetes. The lower line denotes the usual lowest values. Occasionally, values were obtained that were even lower, but no explanation was at hand for these paradoxical results. Our knowledge had not been sufficiently advanced to account for *low* values. The dotted line indicates the normal renal threshold. When the blood sugar rises above this value, the excess sugar spills over into the urine in an attempt by the kidneys to restore the blood sugar to its optimum value.

The Glucose Tolerance Test may be influenced by the patient's previous eating.[24] If he has been taking large amounts of fatty foods, the tolerance will tend to be low—the blood sugar level will tend to be higher. If he has been eating more of the carbohydrate foods, however, his tolerance will tend to be higher—the rise in blood sugar level will not be so great.

Because of this variable, the Exton-Rose Test is being used more extensively.[25] In this modification of the Glucose Tolerance Test, the fasting blood sugar is taken, after which the patient drinks only 50 grams of glucose in solution. Thirty minutes later his blood is drawn again, and another 50-gram glucose solution is administered. A third blood sample is

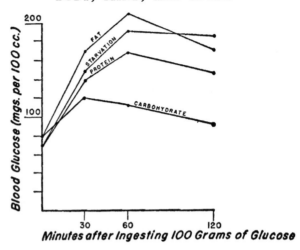

4—*Effect of Diet on the Glucose Tolerance Test*

This chart shows the effect of an earlier meal on the Glucose Tolerance Test. The level of blood sugar depends on the supply of sugar
coming from the stomach, and its removal by the liver under the influence of insulin. Carbohydrate stimulates the production of insulin,
while fat depresses that process. Protein feeding has an effect similar
to that of carbohydrate, since 56 per cent of protein is converted into
glucose during digestion; but this effect, as is to be expected, is less
than that of the direct feeding of straight carbohydrates. In starvation
the stored body fats are consumed as food; the effect would be similar
to that of fat feeding, but to a lesser degree.

taken after another thirty minutes. This test is not significantly influenced by any previous dietary habits. Normally,
the fasting blood sugar lies between 80 and 120 mg. per 100
cc. of blood. The blood taken half an hour later should not be
more than 75 milligrams richer in sugar. The third blood
sample should not be more than 5 milligrams higher than the
second. The urine samples should all be sugar free. This test
is easier on both patient and laboratory, since only three
blood samples are required instead of five.

The stimulus to the patient's islands of Langerhans that
makes them secrete insulin is a rise in blood sugar.[26] In the
Exton-Rose Test the first dose of glucose causes the patient's

[40]

insulin apparatus to produce some of the hormone. When the second portion of sugar is given, there is so much insulin available that the blood sugar should not rise much. In some cases it even falls. In diabetes, however, the insulin apparatus is so sluggish that not enough insulin is secreted to prevent the second dose of glucose from raising the blood sugar level.

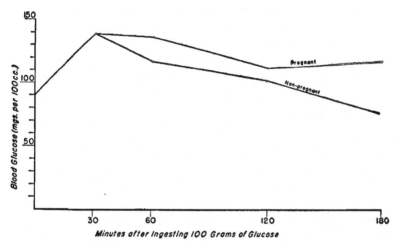

5—*Effect of Pregnancy on the Glucose Tolerance Curve*

The upper curve indicates the average findings in fifty-one pregnant women; the lower, the average of 300 nonpregnant women. None of either group was diabetic.

The glucose tolerance curve also is affected by pregnancy. While the first part of the curve is not changed significantly, the rise is prolonged.[27] We shall have occasion to refer to this fact later.

In normal, healthy operation, the various parts of the body expend the sugar which the blood supplies to them. The blood sugar level then falls, and this drop stimulates the secretions of the adrenal cortex. These substances (cortisone, cortin, etc.) induce an action antithetical to that of insulin. Carried to the liver by the blood, they there effect the re-

[41]

conversion of stored glycogen to glucose. It is the balance between insulin and the adrenal cortical hormones, then, which keeps the blood sugar between the normal levels to which the body's functions are adapted.

The medulla, the inner portion of the adrenal glands, secretes adrenalin, which also induces an action antagonistic to that of insulin. Like the cortical hormones of the same glands, it causes the liver to convert glycogen back to glucose. Unlike the cortical hormones, however, adrenalin is not used in the moment-to-moment operation of the body. Adrenalin acts suddenly and in spurts. It is an emergency hormone, called upon when there is a great demand for energy. It prepares the animal for "fight or flight," when its muscles require large amounts of fuel. Adrenalin also quickens the pulse rate, so that more blood is pumped to all parts of the body. It raises the blood pressure, so that the muscles are flooded with blood containing more fuel for the emergency.

The liver is unique among organs in that it has a double blood supply. Not only does it receive the discharged blood from the digestive tract, pancreas, and spleen through the portal vein, but it is also connected with the general circulation by the hepatic artery. The cortical hormones get to the liver through the hepatic artery, since the veins leaving the adrenal glands are not connected with the portal vein but with the general venous system.

The liver is not the only storage for glycogen. This function is shared with the muscles. The changes from glucose to glycogen and back again take place in the muscles just as they do in the liver and under the same circumstances and stimuli. But most of this action occurs in the liver.

Compare the operation of the human body to that of an automobile. Let the gasoline tank represent the liver, the carburetor the insulin apparatus. When we eat, we fill our liver with body fuel—sugar converted into glycogen. We now are able to "drive" our body for several hours without refueling, while our insulin apparatus regulates the proper mixture—maintains the proper blood sugar level.

Should the insulin supply be inadequate, however, the liver cannot effectively convert sugar to glycogen. Too much sugar is then washed into the blood stream. The blood sugar level rises and remains high. This is diabetes. Thanks to Dr. Banting the diabetic's insulin deficiency can be made up with insulin from the pancreas of a deceased cow. But without injections of insulin—like the automobile that has been "choked" too much—the diabetic body is trying to run on too rich a mixture.

There is an opposite condition in both cars and people. The mixture may be too *weak*. The blood sugar level remains too *low*, because the body's islands of Langerhans supply the liver with too *much* insulin. This is hyperinsulinism.

Hyperinsulinism was discovered two years after Banting had solved the diabetic's major problem. We know now that there are many more sufferers from this "newest" disease, or condition, than there are diabetics. The discovery of hyperinsulinism opened one more tightly closed door. Through it there blazes new light into the dark corners of our ignorance of many things. This new awareness, its significance, and its hope are the subject matter of the remainder of this book.

3

—And the New: Hyperinsulinism

"MEN IN WHITE"—INSULIN SHOCK *vs.* DIABETIC COMA—SEALE HARRIS—THE SIXHOUR GLUCOSE TOLERANCE TEST—THE FOUR CONDITIONS OF HYPERINSULINISM—"THE STEPCHILD OF MEDICINE"—HYPERINSULINISM'S DISGUISES—CAFFEINE—TREATMENT: THE HYPERINSULINISM DIET

IN THE children's ward of a big city hospital the beds are screened off from each other, giving a meager degree of privacy to each patient. Behind one such screen a little girl of ten lies back with eyes closed. Her skin is pale and clammy. She is a diabetic and she has suddenly lost consciousness. Her distracted parents stand beside the bed. A student nurse is speaking rapidly on the telephone.

"South 210, calling Dr. Ferguson. At once!"

The mother is frightened by her child's ghastly pallor. The father paces about, nervously demanding of no one in particular, "Where is Cunningham?" the family physician. "Why isn't he here?"

Presently Dr. Cunningham comes in. He is a dignified and impressive-looking gentleman. He wears a goatee, a pincenez, and has a throaty voice. He is just a bit too much of the professional. He belongs to a vanishing species, much rarer today than it used to be.

"What's happened here?" he asks Barbara, the young student nurse.

She tells him crisply, "Complete collapse. About two minutes ago."

Dr. Cunningham asks to see the chart, which she hands him. With pompous deliberation he looks at it, frowns, shakes his head, and remarks, "H'm. This is bad!" He picks up the child's wrist to take her pulse. He closes his eyes.

Barbara starts to tell him, "Pulse is barely—" but he silences her.

"Let me have my stethoscope," Dr. Cunningham tells Barbara. He takes the instrument and listens to the child's heart. Then he announces, "Diabetic coma."

The child's parents are so upset that Dr. Cunningham banishes them to the hall outside the ward. He then has the young student nurse prepare 40 units of insulin and 50 grams of glucose for an immediate injection.

After our discussion of the coma of acidosis, it is probable that you agree with Dr. Cunningham's diagnosis, that little Dorothy Smith has gone into a coma from which she can be revived only by a prompt injection of insulin. If so, you are just as mistaken as Dr. Cunningham. The little girl has not sunk into the coma of diabetic acidosis. She has collapsed suddenly into the stupor of insulin shock. Additional insulin will probably kill little Dorothy Smith whose parents wait in anguish out in the hall.

Barbara is dimly aware of this, and when ordered to prepare the insulin injection, she protests, "But, sir, Dr. Ferguson advised against insulin."

As Dr. Ferguson is only the hospital intern, while Cunningham is the family physician, this strikes Cunningham as a piece of impertinence of which only a student nurse

[45]

could be guilty. Indignantly he exclaims, "Ferguson? You'll please take your orders from me."

Fortunately for the patient, Ferguson comes in at this moment. He looks at the child and remarks, "I was afraid of shock." An argument follows in which the young intern tries hard to be respectful to the older man who outranks him in the hierarchy of medicine. "I beg your pardon, Doctor, but isn't insulin contraindicated here?"

"No. It's our last chance," says Cunningham stubbornly.

Aware of the young life that ebbs away with each passing second, Ferguson persists, "Doctor, I mean no offense, but I've studied this case history, and it looks like shock, not coma." Cunningham denies it. "But the clinical picture is so clear-cut," Ferguson goes on, urgency creeping into his voice. "Look at the patient. She's pale, cold, clammy. Temperature subnormal. She's complained of hunger. Sudden onset."

Cunningham is annoyed. "Suppose you let me handle the case, young man." He directs the nurse to prepare the child's arm for the injection. She does so.

With helpless despair Ferguson watches Cunningham take up the loaded syringe. Ferguson knows it is loaded with death, a murder weapon. He places his hand on Cunningham's arm and pleads with him, "Please, Doctor! Call one of the other men. Ask them . . . anybody."

"There is no time," Cunningham says coldly. "Take your hand off," he orders, his urbanity cracking a little.

"That insulin is going to prove fatal," says Ferguson.

"Get out of here, will you? I don't want any interruption." Cunningham is getting angry now.

Then, like so many young people who have defied a superior to save a life or gain some equally vital victory, Ferguson makes that split-second decision. Without conscious heroism he risks his career by taking the insulin-loaded syringe from Cunningham's hand and squirting its contents on the floor.

[46]

Cunningham sputters with outraged indignation, "Why did you do that, you fool?"

Ferguson ignores him. He has taken command. It is as if the older man were no longer in the room. With cool efficiency the young intern proceeds with what he knows must be done with all possible speed. He is giving a preview of the sort of doctor he is to be. He will grow with his times, not stagnate as Cunningham has stagnated. He will never take himself more seriously than the situation that happens to confront him.

"Nurse, shock position," Ferguson commands. Barbara moves quickly and raises the foot of the bed. Ferguson looks out from behind the screen and calls out to another nurse, "Sterile glucose, quick, and a 30-cc. syringe." Barbara tells him that she has glucose ready, 50 grams of it. "Half of that will do," he tells her. Then, to the other nurse, he calls, "Never mind the glucose. A hypo of adrenalin. And some hot packs and blankets."

By now Cunningham has sufficiently recovered from the shock of having a mere intern brush him aside to fulminate, "What do you think you're doing? I'll have you brought up before the medical board. I'll have you thrown out of this hospital."

"All right," says Ferguson. "Have me thrown out. I don't give a damn!" And he doesn't. He is busy saving a life. He goes right ahead. After the nurse has swabbed the patient's arm with alcohol, he injects the glucose and then the adrenalin. He and the nurse apply the hot packs and cover the little girl with blankets.

All the while, Cunningham is fuming. "You'll pay for this, young man. The patient's life is in your hands."

Ferguson doesn't seem to have heard. "That's about all we can do," he tells Barbara.

"You report downstairs, at once!" Cunningham orders. But Ferguson and Barbara stand strained, tense, watching the patient. After a long moment the little girl raises her hand to her forehead and opens her eyes. She looks at Ferguson who leans toward her. Very faintly she says, "Dr. George, I'm thirsty."

The battle is won. A life is saved.

This scene actually took place, only on the stage of a theater. We have transcribed it from Sidney Kingsley's fine play, *Men in White*,° in which he so skillfully probed the anatomy of the medical profession.

During the twenty-eight years that insulin has been used in the treatment of diabetes, many patients have suffered occasional insulin shocks. Some of them have died of shock. This condition would come about when an overdose of insulin was given or when a meal was unduly delayed. Another cause of insulin shock was exercise. It was said that a game of tennis or golf was equivalent, in effect, to 15 units of insulin. By quickening the metabolic processes of the body, exercise enables the patient to get along with less insulin. Trouble arises when the diabetic takes his insulin and then indulges in some activity for which he has made no provision by subtracting some insulin from his usual quota.

When the medical profession was first wrestling with the problems of regulating the dosage of insulin, mistakes would sometimes occur. Occasionally, too much insulin was prescribed for the actual needs of the patient—either in error, or because the patient did something, such as exercise, which reduced the need, or again because the patient's improvement made his requirements smaller. The subsequent drop in blood sugar instituted by the insulin progressed too far. The resultant physical condition is known as insulin shock.

Insulin shock is ushered in with startling symptoms. The patient feels faint and hungry and soon experiences palpitation of the heart and a cold sweat. He complains of a severe headache and often "sees double." Now the signs follow the symptoms.

° Copyright, 1933, by Sidney Kingsley.

(A *symptom* is experienced by the patient and described to the physician; a *sign* is observed by the doctor himself. A headache, for example, is a symptom, while a rash is an obvious sign.) As the signs of insulin shock become evident, the patient begins to tremble, his gait is unsteady. Some victims exhibit a muttering delirium. (At times they have been picked up by police for alleged drunkenness.) In spite of feeling famished, a patient occasionally will be assailed with nausea and vomit the food he has taken to relieve his hunger. Eventually the victim of insulin shock goes into a deep stupor. Some patients have convulsions in the midst of their stupor.

The deep stupor of insulin shock—to the confusion of *Men in White's* Dr. Cunningham and others—looks exactly like the coma of diabetic acidosis. Both are states of unconsciousness. To some, "stupor" may indicate a state of unconsciousness a shade less profound than "coma," or again the words may be used properly as synonymous. In medical usage, however, the two words are not the same. Though stupor and coma describe conditions identical in appearance, their cause is different. The American Diabetes Association has recommended calling the unconsciousness of insulin shock *stupor,* reserving the term *coma* for that of diabetic acidosis. This avoids confusion. There is only one physical sign to differentiate between the two: in coma the eyeballs tend to be soft; in stupor, they do not. In addition, of course, the odor of acetone cannot be detected on the breath in stupor.

In most cases there was little difficulty in making the diagnosis. If the patient had been under treatment in the hospital it was quite simple. Coma usually comes on gradually, while insulin shock strikes with lightning-like rapidity. When an unconscious patient was brought to a hospital, however, considerable laboratory work often was required to determine which condition was present. A low blood sugar ostensibly indicated stupor. It was entirely possible, however (and it actually did happen), that, as the result of an overzealous treatment with insulin, a patient in coma would be shifted into insulin shock so rapidly that the fleeting interval of consciousness might be missed. When a patient is unconscious, the urine is taken, by catheterizing the bladder, to see if acetone is present; it should not be in the urine in shock. But the urine may have been in the bladder for some time. The presence of acetone might mean that the patient *had been* in acidosis—and not necessarily that his present state of unconsciousness was due to it. In an actual case, a patient felt himself getting drowsy. He realized that he was in mild acidosis and he took some insulin to correct the condition. In his slightly befuddled state, however, he took enough insulin to give him shock, and was rushed to the hospital completely unconscious. His urine contained acetone. It took a nicety of judgment on the part of the intern to diagnose the case as stupor and not the coma of diabetic acidosis.

Not every patient was always as lucky as this one or the little girl in *Men in White*. Not all interns were so intelligent, and few were daring enough to disobey orders. In another actual case, the patient had insulin pumped into her repeatedly because, as her poorly informed doctor explained, "She wouldn't come out of her coma." He gave her several hundred units within two hours. By the time the resident physician responded to the frantic calls of the visiting doctor, the patient was dead. The resident removed some blood from the corpse's heart, and found that the sample contained less than 15 milligrams of glucose per 100 cubic centimeters of blood! The private physician had been using insulin for the first time. He had not learned about it in medical school, nor had he attended any of the hospital's staff meetings at which insulin had been discussed. He had killed his patient with ignorance. This incident occurred many years ago. Today such ignorance is utterly impossible.

Although supposedly conquered in one direction, ignorance frequently persists, or arises elsewhere. Recently, for example, a diabetic was prevailed upon by a food faddist to dispense with those "poisonous injections of insulin." He was assured that with the proper dietary treatment he would be rid of his diabetes for good. First, he was to fast for a few days. Three days later when his family called in his doctor, the patient was in coma. The diabetic's insulin apparatus was so badly damaged that it manufactured practically no insulin at all. The cultist had not known that this patient was a "total diabetic." He also probably did not know that starvation alone can produce a mild acidosis even in a normal person. After no food is eaten for some time, a person eats up his glycogen stores. Then he consumes his own body fat. There being no carbohydrate to burn with that fat, acidosis occurs, as in diabetes. In the normal fasting individual, the acidosis is usually mild. But if long continued, as in famine or the deliberate starvation in the German prisoner of war and Displaced Persons camps of World War II, the sufferers die in coma. In the diabetic's case just described, the added burden of severe diabetes rushed matters along. After a liberal dose of insulin and glucose, however, the patient revived.

It was important for diabetic patients to recognize the preliminary symptoms of insulin shock. Many physicians deliberately administered slight overdoses of insulin toward the end of their patient's period of hospitalization. In this way the diabetic would become acquainted with the symptoms while still where countermeasures could be taken promptly. The patient would then be given some sugar or sweetened orange juice, and the premonition of shock—a feeling of intense hunger and lightheadedness—would vanish. The diabetic would be told what had been done, and warned to eat something sweet whenever he felt similar symptoms in the future. During the 1920's all diabetics carried a few pieces of sugar with them for emergency use against a possible insulin reaction.

After Protamine-Zinc-Insulin came on the market, the shock

[51]

problem changed its complexion. At first it was serious and
baffling. Frequently diabetes specialists would be called early
in the morning to see a patient who had been switched recently from insulin to Protamine-Zinc-Insulin. The patient
would be found in the stupor of insulin shock. A sterile glucose
solution would be injected intravenously, the patient would
revive almost immediately, and the doctor would leave.
Within almost a matter of minutes the patient would be in
shock again. The doctor would have to return and administer
another injection of glucose. What had happened was soon
understood. Protamine-Zinc-Insulin has its peak action about
twenty-four hours after the injection. The first shock coincided
with this peak. The first glucose injection took care of only
that insulin which was circulating in the patient's blood at that
time. But there was still a depot of unused insulin at the site
of the previous day's P.Z.I. injection. When more of this
residual insulin was absorbed, the blood sugar again fell. In
order to prevent a repetition of this process, sweet drinks
would be administered for a number of hours. At times it was
necessary to administer sterile glucose intravenously by a slow
drip lasting for as long as twenty-four hours. This was necessary, for example, in the case of a patient who inadvertently
bought a bottle of P.Z.I. twice as strong as had been prescribed.

Today such accidents are rare. We have learned that it is
safer to undertreat, rather than risk overdosage. We now attempt to keep the blood sugar as nearly normal as possible. We
have learned to be not quite so concerned by some sugar in
the urine. Our aim is to keep it down to 15 grams (half an
ounce) a day. But even properly administered P.Z.I. may
sometimes produce a slight insulin reaction with very mild
symptoms. In such cases the patient may be a bit tired or have
a headache on awakening, but this disappears soon after
he has eaten breakfast. In addition he may be fatigued before other meals.

[52]

We have dwelt at some length on insulin shock because its symptoms are important to the rest of our story.

In 1924, only one year after insulin was in general use, Dr. Seale Harris, then professor of medicine at the University of Alabama, noticed that many people who were not diabetic and who were not taking insulin nevertheless experienced some of the symptoms of insulin shock.

Seale Harris knew that other ductless glands can be over- or underactive. Diseases resulting from abnormalities of the thyroid gland, for example, were known centuries before we had any knowledge of ductless glands as such, or of their functions. Something has been known about Graves' Disease (toxic goiter) since early in the nineteenth century. This we now know to be *hyper*thyroidism. Its victims have a rapid pulse and elevated blood pressure; they lose weight and are extremely nervous. In the sixteenth century, Paracelsus wrote about *myxedema*. Myxedema (cretinism in children) is *hypo*thyroidism and is characterized by a slow pulse, low blood pressure, obesity, and a phlegmatic disposition bordering on and occasionally reaching torpor.

Why, then, shouldn't the islands of Langerhans—the insulin apparatus—be subject to similar aberrations? Diabetes mellitus was just such an aberration. It was *hypo*insulinism. Harris investigated those nondiabetics who had symptoms of insulin shock, and found their blood sugar level to be abnormally low. He further found that if their blood sugar level dropped abruptly, these patients were prone to a more extreme attack of the symptoms of insulin shock.

Seale Harris reported on this matter in September, 1924,[1] and called the condition *hyper*insulinism. He maintained that it resulted from an excessive secretion of the hormone by the patient's own insulin apparatus.

To diagnose the hyperinsulinism condition Dr. Harris devised a modification of the Glucose Tolerance Test used in diabetes.[2] This consisted of prolonging to six hours the period during which the blood is analyzed for sugar and drawing the blood samples at hourly intervals. Harris noticed that all his hyperinsulinism patients showed drops of sugar concentration as the analysis time was lengthened. Such a drop does not occur in the normal body.

By means of this six-hour test, Harris was able to verify another startling observation. In certain diabetics the symptoms alternated between those of diabetes and those of spontaneous insulin shock. When given to these patients, the six-hour Glucose Tolerance Test revealed curves which for the first three hours were similar to those of any other diabetic. After that, however, the sugar level took a sharp dip to the levels indicating hyperinsulinism. If these patients were tested in the standard manner there was nothing in the results to indicate that they were not pure diabetics. But the new six-hour test dramatically drew attention to a hitherto unknown condition, for which Harris coined the term *dys*insulinism. To explain this strange condition which partakes of the nature of two exactly opposite conditions, Harris postulated a time delay in the secretion of insulin in response to a metabolic demand, followed by an overcompensation which floods the blood with an excess of insulin. Insulin secretion is roughly analogous to rainfall. The normal person's insulin secretion is like the normal rainfall of the temperate zone. Just as rain occurs in moderate amounts every few days, so insulin is secreted at frequent intervals in response to the metabolic demand, and no more. The diabetic is a desert dweller. Like the desert's rainfall, the secretion of insulin is insufficient for life. Hyperinsulinism, on the other hand, is the continuous downpour in a region of endlessly soaking rains. Dysinsulinism is the parched desert pining for rain and getting it from time to time in a torrential flood that does much harm and no good.

While *hyperglycemia* (literally *too much sugar* in the blood) may result from other causes, diabetes always produces

[54]

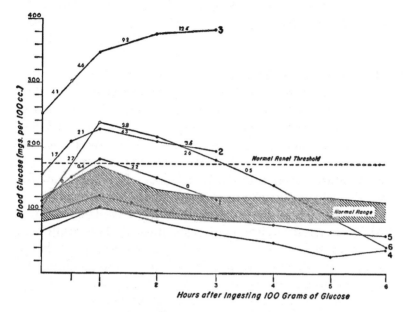

Hours after Ingesting 100 Grams of Glucose

6—*The Six-hour Glucose Tolerance Test*

For comparison, actual cases involving the shorter test have been included to demonstrate diabetic curves. The small figures above the segments of each curve indicate the amounts of glucose (in grams) excreted during that period. The different curves are:

1. An exceedingly mild case of diabetes. Notice that the fasting blood glucose level is quite normal. The patient was, for all practical purposes, only potentially diabetic. He need only avoid excessive amounts of sweets.

2. A moderately severe case of diabetes. This patient must take insulin.

3. An extremely severe diabetic. This sometimes is called "total diabetes," for the patient has practically no insulin of his own. The rise in blood sugar persists for several hours. This patient requires more than 100 units of insulin a day.

4. Manifest hyperinsulinism. This patient had the classical symptoms of hyperinsulinism. She "blacked out" on many occasions. It will be noticed that the level at the sixth hour is higher than at the fifth. This rise probably is due to stimulation of the adrenal glands by the great drop in blood sugar, after which the adrenal hormones begin to raise that level.

5. Subclinical hyperinsulinism. This patient had none of the usual symptoms of hyperinsulinism. She complained only of a state of mental depression which yielded completely to the dietary treatment.

6. Dysinsulinism. If this test had been made for only three hours,

[55]

an excess of blood sugar. Similarly, *hypoglycemia* (*too little sugar*) may result from conditions other than hyperinsulinism, but hyperinsulinism always produces a deficiency in blood sugar.

In 1926 Gray and Femmster reported the case of a diabetic woman who gave birth to an apparently normal child.[3] The infant soon died in insulin shock. The fetus had developed in an environment that was hyperglycemic—overrich in blood sugar. While there is no direct connection between the maternal and fetal blood vessels, the sugar in a pregnant woman's blood diffuses freely into the fetus' blood. To compensate for this, the cells in the islands of Langerhans of the developing fetus multiplied in excess of what would have been normal, had its prenatal environment been normal. The result was that when the child was born and its connection with the mother's overrich blood sugar level severed, too much insulin was secreted and the baby died of severe insulin shock.

Diabetic mothers greatly tend to abort before term. The babies usually are quite large, but modern practice avoids this complication by delivering the babies prematurely. There may be other complications, however, as a result of frequent disturbances of the sex hormones in diabetics. This condition sometimes causes the development of congenital defects in the child, such as missing digits, webbed fingers, or club feet.

In 1927, at the Mayo Clinic in Rochester, Minnesota, Doctors Wilder, Allen, Power, and Robertson reported a case that has since become famous.[4] The patient was a physician, not diabetic, who had many attacks of insulin shock. These came on with increasing frequency and severity. He had to be given increasing sugar at increasingly frequent intervals. He had to be watched in his sleep and awakened when he twitched, so that he could replenish his blood sugar. Although

the diagnosis would have been diabetes. On prolonging the test, however, the blood sugar level dropped precipitously after the fourth hour. This curve was obtained on a patient with asthma and diabetes.

his case was studied thoroughly, nothing could be done for him and he died. An autopsy revealed a hitherto unknown condition: a malignant tumor—a cancer—of the islands of Langerhans. These diseased cells had thrown off secondary growths which, having traveled through the lymph or blood, had taken root in other organs of the body. (This process is known medically as *metastasis*. A metastasis from a malignancy has the nature of the parent growth.) When these secondary growths were extracted with acidulated water and the extract was injected into rabbits, the animals went into insulin shock and there was a great lowering of their blood sugar levels. The patient had suffered from a newly discovered type of cancer—*insuloma*. He had been manufacturing insulin all over his body.

The case was important for several reasons. It had revealed a new type of cancer. It had established one cause of hyperinsulinism—a malignant tumor of the islands of Langerhans in the pancreas. And it had shown that insulin could be secreted in other parts of the body than the pancreas. The case helped Seale Harris in reasoning about the problems of hyperinsulinism. There were many points of similarity between the case at the Mayo Clinic and those he had seen in Birmingham. They differed only in severity and in the fatal outcome of the Rochester case.

In 1929 Graham operated to remove a tumor of the islands of Langerhans which differed from the latter case in that it was not malignant. This growth did not expel small portions to travel in the body fluids.[5] Allen O. Whipple has thoroughly investigated these benign tumors of the islands of the pancreas. He has operated on many patients afflicted with them and has reported many cures. Whipple and others have also described a similar condition in which, while there is no tumor or group of tumors in the pancreas, there is a generalized, diffused enlargement of the islands of Langerhans. By removing a part of the left end or tail of the pancreas—

the region in which the islands are generally most numerous —the patient can be restored to health.[6]

Thus we have four similar conditions of hyperinsulinism, differing in cause, severity, and treatment necessary to effect a cure. The severest and, fortunately, by far the rarest form of hyperinsulinism is that caused by malignant insuloma. Treatment is ineffectual; as in many types of visceral cancer, mortality is 100 per cent. The second variety is caused by a benign and removable tumor of the islands of Langerhans. One or two lumps grow in the pancreas and these secrete too much insulin. (Sometimes they can be felt through the abdominal wall. At operation, if on the surface of the pancreas, the tumors can be seen as lilac-colored lumps of from 1 to 2 centimeters in diameter and partly protruding from the surface of the gland. When they are deeper they can be felt through the softer tissue of the normal portions of the gland in which they are imbedded.) These tumors can be removed by surgery. Whipple requires that three conditions be present in the patient before he will operate: the fasting blood sugar must be below 50 mg. per 100 cc. of blood; the frequent attacks must be accompanied by an extremely low blood sugar level; the attacks must be completely relieved by administration of glucose, with the blood sugar level rising as the symptoms subside. Under these conditions Whipple not only indicates that he favors operation but seems to consider it essential "to prevent the benign tumors from becoming malignant or causing mental deterioration as a result of keeping the brain tissue undernourished." (On June 11, 1951, Dr. Whipple received the American Medical Association's distinguished service award for his work.)

The third kind of hyperinsulinism is that due to a generalized enlargement of the island tissue without any concentration into any demonstrable lump. This type can be cured by the removal of part of the pancreas. It should, however, be given medical care for some time before operation, since many such cases have yielded to nonsurgical treatment.

The fourth and by far the most common form of hyperinsulinism is the one that Harris called "functional hyperinsulinism." In functional hyperinsulinism there apparently is no demonstrable anatomical change in the islands of Langerhans in size, structure, or number, at least as far as present methods of investigation reveal. But these apparently normal glands nevertheless produce more insulin than they should. Harris found this fourth type of hyperinsulinism to be even more prevalent in his experience than its opposite, diabetes. He devised a diet to overcome this condition.[7]

First indicated in 1924 and reported on again in 1932 and 1936, Seale Harris' great discovery is still only vaguely known to most rank-and-file practitioners. According to Dr. Martin Grotjahn, eminent Los Angeles psychiatrist, it has been "the Stepchild of Medicine." To this day many prominent investigators challenge the Harris findings and conclusions, or ignore them. This, in spite of the fact that by the most conservative estimate there are well over a million persons suffering from hyperinsulinism in the United States, and probably from ten to thirty times that number. These are the wretched people who usually are treated ineffectually for everything under the sun except the condition that afflicts them. Persons who at last were found to be suffering from hyperinsulinism have been treated for coronary thrombosis and other heart ailments, brain tumor, epilepsy, gall bladder disease, appendicitis, hysteria, and every sort of neurosis. They have been told repeatedly that their trouble is "all in the mind" and sent to the psychoanalyst.

Some of the eminent surgeons who deny or doubt the existence of functional hyperinsulinism nevertheless have been forced to admit that they have operated on a patient (who had exhibited all the signs and symptoms of hyperinsulinism) to perform their pancreatotomy, and found neither a tumor to remove nor any hypertrophy or other anatomical indication that there was anything the matter with the patient's islands of Langerhans! This has happened not once but several times. As a result, it has been suggested that perhaps in such cases the tumor is too small to be seen!

The normal conservatism of the medical profession, the "cultural lag," the inability of the hard-pressed present-day practitioner to keep up with the literature—a condition made more acute than ever by the demands on his services during World War II, which came at the very time when Harris' findings would have been absorbed under peacetime conditions—all these considerations help to explain the stepchild treatment of hyperinsulinism. But they do not altogether suffice. The best explanation of the anomaly is found in a letter from Dr. Sidney A. Portis of the University of Illinois, who has made important contributions to the knowledge of hyperinsulinism (which will be discussed in a later chapter). Dr. Portis suggests that the trouble with hyperinsulinism is that it cannot be packaged, publicized, and sold over the counter in a drugstore. The "miracle drugs," starting with insulin itself, have caught the imagination of the public. They are something tangible which can be obtained in a bottle, and the public's reaction to them has in turn affected the physicians' attitude. There is no glamorous cure for hyperinsulinism that can be bought in a package. Its diagnosis and treatment demand pains from the physician and sacrifices from the patient, who must give up candy, sugar, pies, alcohol, coffee, and sometimes smoking. Being human, doctors much prefer to write a prescription for a miracle drug than to order the execution of habits of self-indulgence hitherto considered quite harmless.

In the end, however, fate has been kinder to Dr. Harris than to many other trail blazers. In 1949 the American Medical Association gave Harris an "achievement award" and caused a medal to be struck in his honor. This signal distinction has been made only a dozen times in the association's century of existence. As the far-reaching consequences of his discovery spread throughout the medical profession and lead to further discoveries and greater understanding, it is to be hoped that other honors and rewards may come to Seale Harris.

Harris called hyperinsulinism the "hunger disease." Others have called it "fatigue" and "chronic fatigue." Hunger, of a most ravenous kind, is certainly the outstanding symptom, while fatigue is undoubtedly a common symptom in many cases. Admittedly, hyperinsulinism is a mouthful. Hypoinsulinism has an easily spoken name in diabetes. Perhaps, hyperinsulinism will in time be known as sugar starvation, for that is what it literally is. Sugar is the fuel of every cell in the body. While most body cells can derive some nourishment from other sources, however, the nourishment of the brain is exclusively glucose. Moreover, unlike some other organs which store sugar, the brain is dependent upon the moment-to-moment blood sugar level for its functioning. Blood sugar, then, is as important to life as the air we breathe; it is sugar which burns in the oxygen we breathe.

Before discussing the signs and symptoms and treatment of hyperinsulinism, however, we must understand how it comes about.

The stimulus to the islands of Langerhans which causes them to pour their secretion into the blood is a rise in blood sugar. It is not the actual level, no matter how high, but the jump in that level. A rise from 80 to 140, for example, has about the same effect as one from 180 to 240. (This effect is well known. It is the basis for the Exton-Rose sugar tolerance test.) When we eat, the processes of digestion convert the food into glucose at the rate of 100 per cent of the carbohydrates, 56 per cent of the proteins, and 10 per cent of the fats. The blood carries the glucose from the intestinal tract into the liver, but there is little insulin in the liver at the time. The sugar passes through the organ largely unchanged and is carried by the general circulation into the pancreas, where the suddenly increased blood sugar level stimulates the islands of Langerhans to produce insulin. This insulin reaches the liver while the major part of the meal is still being digested, enabling the liver to remove the excess glucose from the blood and in the process charge itself with glycogen. In a few hours the situation is brought back to about the initial condition. During the interval between meals as we do work (mental and/or physical) and thus expend the blood sugar, the adrenal corticle hormones induce the liver to break up the glycogen into sugar, which in turn is fed into the blood to maintain the proper level.

In diabetes the damaged islands of Langerhans cannot produce enough insulin for the body's requirements, and the liver is unable to remove enough glucose (by converting it into glycogen) coming to it from the digestive tract. The blood sugar level raised by the conversion of foods to sugar remains high. If the level rises high enough, it pours over the dam of the renal threshold and spills into the urine in the body's futile attempt to correct the real evil—high blood sugar.

In hyperinsulinism we have the exactly opposite state of affairs. The islands of Langerhans are *too sensitive*. In response to the metabolic demand, they secrete too much insulin. The liver converts too much sugar into starch, leaving too little in the circulating blood. The net late result of eating a meal is a drop in blood sugar. The sufferer from this condition is always hungry and no amount of eating will keep the level of his blood sugar where it belongs.

The symptoms of manifest hyperinsulinism are hunger, weakness, fatigue, anxiety and nervousness, crying spells, a feeling of tremulousness, incoordination for fine movements, mental disturbances such as confusion, disorientation, and a low, muttering delirium, and, in most severe cases, stupor.

It will be remembered that a drop in blood sugar causes

[62]

the adrenal cortex to secrete its hormones to bring the level back to normal by breaking down some of the starch in the liver. If the blood sugar level falls low enough, the emergency part of the adrenal glands goes into action, and adrenalin enters the blood. This brings on the tachycardia or palpitation of the heart, flushing, and convulsions. These symptoms are identical with those of the diabetic who has been overdosed with insulin, but in hyperinsulinism the offending agent is the patient's own insulin. Usually, the most severe cases are accompanied by the lowest blood sugar levels.

This is by no means a complete list of hyperinsulinism symptoms. Several lists compiled by various authorities who studied the matter in the years immediately following Harris' 1936 report are much longer; each of the three most complete lists would cover this page. Hyperinsulinism wears the symptomatic disguises of many other ailments. It is no wonder that inexperienced doctors have difficulty diagnosing hyperinsulinism. The matter is made even more difficult by the fact that there is only one *sign* of hyperinsulinism—a tenderness in the left upper quadrant of the abdomen—to which Harris called attention in 1933.

The surest way to determine the presence of the condition is by means of the six-hour Glucose Tolerance Test. But it must be the *six-hour* test and not a shorter one, since the latter may not be sufficient to permit the blood sugar level drop to occur.

The malady develops insidiously. At first there is an occasional slight feeling of lightheadedness. Then, in the course of a few years, perhaps, the frequency and severity of the attacks increase markedly, and the patient is assailed by ravenous hunger and utter fatigue. Soon other strange and disquieting symptoms creep up on him. There was a woman of thirty-three, for example, who suffered several attacks of complete unconsciousness. (This was in 1935, before the invention of the electroencephalograph, the electric device which records the "brain waves" and from which we can now diagnose and even localize brain tumors and other conditions within the skull.) A competent brain specialist diagnosed this woman's condition as a possible brain tumor, and preparations were made for an exploratory operation. Fortunately, however, a Glucose Tolerance Test was given first and the correct diagnosis of hyperinsulinism was clearly revealed. The operation was not performed, and the patient has been in good health ever since the proper treatment was instituted.

The attacks tend to occur if a meal is delayed or if any undue exertion depletes the store of sugar in the blood. Sometimes they will occur after an illness which subjects the body to unusually great wear. A salesman who traveled about the city in his car had been ill with grippe. Because he had not called on his customers for several weeks, he now rushed about to get in as many calls as possible. One day he went without luncheon. At about four in the afternoon he felt dizzy and pulled over to the curb and parked his car. It was fortunate that he stopped, because he suddenly slumped over the wheel. The usual crowd gathered. A call was put in for an ambulance, but the man revived before it arrived. (This incident occurred early in the postwar years before hospitals had resumed their prewar practice of having an intern ride in every ambulance.) Urged by the ambulance attendant, the man drove to the hospital where an intern made a diagnosis of coronary heart disease. This was not confirmed by the electrocardiogram, but then a negative reading can occur even in the face of a severe coronary thrombosis. To play safe, the patient was kept in bed for the usual six weeks. After his discharge he had another attack, and this time he was examined by an alert physician who suspected hyperinsulinism. The Glucose Tolerance Test confirmed the diagnosis. The patient responded to treatment and has had no recurrence in four years.

[64]

Another case involved a man who had a luncheon appointment with a business prospect. An important sale was to be consummated over the table. When the man found that his guest had not arrived at the restaurant, he decided to wait for him outside in his car. It was a very hot day. The guest was delayed for two hours. Suddenly the waiting man blacked out. An ambulance was called and he was taken to the hospital. Physical examination and the electrocardiograph ruled out the suspected coronary thrombosis. The case was first labeled "heat prostration," in spite of the fact that the victim did not have the high temperature that usually goes with heat stroke. The Glucose Tolerance Test, however, revealed the true state of affairs. The man was treated for hyperinsulinism and recovered completely.

One hesitates to rob Dr. Harris of any credit that is his due, but actually he was in a strategic position to discover hyperinsulinism. As he pointed out, overindulgence in caffeine is a common cause for the condition. Harris conducted his research in Birmingham, Alabama, the heart of the South, where various beverages consisting of sweetened and flavored water "spiked" with caffeine are water substitutes. Hyperinsulinism may be induced in persons predisposed to the condition by the very combination of caffeine and sugar found in these beverages.

Overindulgence in sweets tends to sensitize the islands of Langerhans by subjecting them to repeated stimulation and exercise. Caffeine stimulates the adrenal cortex to produce more of its hormones, which in turn induce the liver to break down glycogen into glucose which flows into the blood stream. This is why a cup of coffee "gives you a lift." Trouble develops because the islands of Langerhans cannot distinguish between the effects of drinking coffee and eating food. They don't know and don't care whether the sugar has come from the food that is being digested or from previously stored glycogen, broken down by the action of the caffeine's stimulus to the adrenal cortex. To the islands of Langerhans sugar is sugar. They go to work to force the blood sugar to its normal level. In the course of time, because of their repeated stimulation, the islands become so sensitive that they overrespond to a normal stimulus.

Anyone trying to lose weight who drinks black coffee to still the pangs of hunger is only making matters worse for himself. The repeated stimulus to the islands of Langerhans makes them more sensitive, and the resultant low blood sugar only makes the rigid diet more onerous. Dieting to reduce is much easier if coffee, as well as caffeine in other forms (such as strong tea, chocolate, and soft drinks containing that alkaloid), is excluded.

What is the rational treatment for hyperinsulinism? It has been suggested that injections of insulin would tend to diminish the sensitivity of the islands of Langerhans by furnishing some of that hormone, and thereby reduce the need for the islands to produce so much. While this would seem logical, it has not proved practicable. We know that the symptoms are due to the cell starvation resulting from a relatively low blood sugar. So, one may say, let's stuff ourselves with sugar. This will relieve an attack. But study of the Glucose Tolerance Test reveals that the net effect of taking sugar is a further drop in blood sugar. The trouble lies in the oversensitive islands of Langerhans. We must deaden them a bit. The diet therefore should be relatively high in fat, since this depresses the activity of the islands of Langerhans. It should be clearly understood, however, that we are considering a diet to *check* such attacks of hyperinsulinism as we have discussed. A lifetime high fat diet would be dangerous since, it should be remembered, it might cause arteriosclerosis or diabetes.

When we arise in the morning we have a relatively low level of sugar in the blood. After breakfast the level rises, stimulating the islands of Langerhans to the production of insulin. In the normal person, as we have already seen, the secreted insulin takes care of the normal excess, and the blood sugar level is kept within the normal range. In the victim of hyperinsulinism, however, too much insulin is secreted and the blood sugar level drops too far. Before it hits bottom, the hyperinsulinism victim should eat again. Thus, the second principle is to take frequent meals. By eating often you eat less each time, so that instead of having three upward and downward wide swings in blood sugar level, you will have six or seven small ones. In time the blood sugar level will tend to smooth out.

Since a sudden rise in blood sugar stimulates the islands of Langerhans, the foods prescribed for the victim of hyper-insulinism should omit the quickly absorbable carbohydrates. This means no sugar, candy, or other sweets, no cake with icing, no pies or other pastry, no ice cream, no honey, no syrup, no grape juice or prune juice. And regrettably, our string of "no's" includes cocktails, wines, cordials, and beer. Finally, if you have hyperinsulinism, you must avoid caffeine as you would the pest. The working girl's standard luncheon-ette breakfast of coffee and Danish is out! It's tough—but not as bad as living in constant misery or blacking out at the wheel of your car.

The diet on the next two pages has been modified slightly from that prescribed by Dr. Harris to make it more palatable to average tastes. There is another diet prescribed by many doctors which achieves similar results. Originally devised by Drs. Conn,[8] it prohibits many of the same things as the Harris diet, differing mainly in being a high protein diet.

We object to the Conn diet for two reasons: First, the average palate rebels against the monotony of an excessive protein diet, and second, so does the average pocketbook—proteins are the most expensive of foods and particularly high at this time.

[67]

DIET FOR HYPERINSULINISM

On Arising—Medium orange, half grapefruit, or 4 ounces of juice.

Breakfast—Fruit or 4 ounces of juice; 1 egg with or without two slices of ham or bacon; ONLY ONE slice of any bread or toast with plenty of butter; beverage.

2 Hours After Breakfast—4 ounces of juice.

Lunch—Meat, fish, cheese, or eggs; salad (large serving of lettuce, tomato, or Waldorf Salad with mayonnaise or French dressing); vegetables if desired; ONLY ONE slice of any bread or toast with plenty of butter; dessert; beverage.

3 Hours After Lunch—8 ounces of milk.

1 Hour Before Dinner—4 ounces of juice.

Dinner—Soup if desired (not thickened with flour); vegetables; liberal portion of meat, fish, or poultry; ONLY ONE slice of bread if desired; dessert; beverage.

2–3 Hours After Dinner—8 ounces of milk.

Every 2 Hours Until Bedtime—4 ounces of milk or a small handful of nuts.

Allowable Vegetables—Asparagus, avocado, beets, broccoli, Brussels sprouts, cabbage, cauliflower, carrots, celery, corn, cucumbers, eggplant, Lima beans, onions, peas, radishes, sauerkraut, squash, string beans, tomatoes, turnips.

Allowable Fruits—Apples, apricots, berries, grapefruit, melons, oranges, peaches, pears, pineapple, tangerines.

May be cooked or raw, with or without cream but without sugar. Canned fruits should be packed in water, not syrup.

Lettuce, mushrooms, and nuts may be taken as freely as desired.

Juice—Any unsweetened fruit or vegetable juice, except grape juice or prune juice.

Beverages—Weak tea (tea ball, not brewed); decaffeinated coffee; coffee substitutes. May be sweetened with saccharin.

Desserts—Fruit, unsweetened gelatin, junket (made from tablets, not mix).

Alcoholic and Soft Drinks—Club soda, *dry* ginger ale, whiskies, and other DISTILLED liquors.

. AVOID ABSOLUTELY—Sugar, candy, and other sweets, such as cake, pie, pastries, sweet custards, puddings, and ice cream.

Caffeine—ordinary coffee, strong brewed tea, beverages containing caffeine. (Your doctor will tell you what these are.)

Potatoes, rice, grapes, raisins, plums, figs, dates, and bananas.

Spaghetti, macaroni, and noodles.

Wines, cordials, cocktails, and beer.

The first feeding on arising starts the body's machinery, and breakfast builds it up to speed. The midmorning juice helps maintain that speed until lunch, while the afternoon milk prevents the late afternoon slowdown, so common in hyperinsulinism. The juice before dinner acts as a governor—takes the edge off the now-ravenous appetite and prevents overeating. Since the diet requires that the patient eat more

[69]

frequently, this juice feeding is important, as surrender to the untempered appetite might result in an excessive weight increase. The additional feedings between dinner and bedtime care for the bodily activities until the machinery again is at rest.

✓This is the diet for all cases of hyperinsulinism. It should be followed for, say, three months. If the symptoms still persist, this may be an indication of a tumor or generalized enlargement in size or number of the islands of Langerhans. These are conditions which may call for an operation, which, if needed, should not be delayed too long. Patients with hyperinsulinism tend to have ravenous appetites, and any resultant obesity would make the operation more difficult.

We have now completed the essentials—what hyperinsulinism is and how it should be treated. The exact opposite of diabetes, it is a condition in which the blood sugar level is relatively low and tends to starve the body's cells, especially the brain cells. It is treated by diet or, if necessary, by surgery. The real story of this multivisaged ailment remains to be told. What happens to us when the cells of our bodies and especially our brains are chronically undernourished? The weakest, most vulnerable cells—those with the lowest resistance—suffer first. These will differ from person to person and from time to time in the same individual, thus producing the almost infinite variety of hyperinsulinism manifestations in different persons, and in the same person at different times of his life. It is these often widely dissimilar manifestations of sugar starvation which explain why hyperinsulinism has remained unknown so long, and why now that we know it, it is so often unrecognized. For it is like that fictional detective, so adept at disguises that no one knew what the real man looked like.

[70]

4

Sneezes, Wheezes, Aches, and Pains

THE ALLERGIES—HAY FEVER—ASTHMA—
RHEUMATIC FEVER—ULCERS, REAL AND
IMAGINARY—SOME CASE HISTORIES

"Now ODORS pleasant to physicians and agreeable to all men or to most sometimes . . . may be unpleasant to one. I know men in health, who directly after the odor of roses have a severe reaction from this, so that they have a headache, or it causes sneezing, or induces such a troublesome itching in the nostrils that they cannot, for a space of two days, restrain themselves from rubbing them." So wrote Leonardo Botallo of Asti in the Piedmont in 1565.[1] This is the first recorded description of what was first called "rose catarrh," later "rose fever," and now is referred to as the grass or spring variety of hay fever.

Hay fever is one of the allergic disorders. These are among the strangest maladies to afflict mankind. Unlike other strange diseases which are usually rare, however, the allergies are quite common. It has been reliably estimated that there are three million hay fever sufferers in the United States.[2] Asthma, eczema, and other allergies are almost as common. The grand total of allergics must approach five million in the United States alone. And they abound in nearly all countries.

[71]

In the centuries after Botallo, many others described hay fever with increasing detail, notably Bostock in 1819. The first to ascribe the cause to plant pollens was Elliotson a few years later. Since then we have accumulated a vast amount of data concerning hay fever and the other allergies, but we still do not know why certain persons should be hypersensitive to substances which are completely harmless to others.

The official name of hay fever is Seasonal Allergic Rhinitis. Chronologically, there are three kinds: the early spring; the late spring and early summer; and the late summer and early fall. The first is caused by hypersensitivity to the pollen of trees; the next to the pollen of grasses; and the third to the pollen of weeds. The dates of these periods vary with latitude, altitude, proximity to water, and prevailing winds, and whether the season itself is early, "normal," or late. Theoretically, one could escape hay fever by starting to move toward the Arctic Circle in spring, keeping ahead of the allergy as it proceeds farther north. The average number of hay fever days per season varies greatly in different parts of the country, from a felicitous zero in Arizona, California, Florida, Oregon, Washington, Nevada, and extreme northwestern Texas, to a baneful 42 days in Dallas, Texas, 41 in Hatteras, North Carolina, 39 in Springfield, Illinois, 38 in Peoria and Kansas City, 37 in Indianapolis and Oklahoma City, and 36 in St. Louis and Omaha. In general it is high throughout the central portions of the country from Texas to Minnesota—33 in Minneapolis, for example, and over a month in most of Tennessee, Kentucky, Ohio, Indiana, and western Pennsylvania and New York. It is 35 in Buffalo in contrast with 20 in New York City, 15 at Coney Island, and only 3 at Lake Saranac. It declines rapidly with altitude. It is far lower at the top of the Empire State Building than in the street below. It is light in most of the Rocky Mountain region and very low in northern Maine and Michigan.

Some unfortunates suffer from all three types of hay fever.

[72]

They start sneezing when the trees bloom in early spring and don't stop until snow flies in the fall. Many persons have two kinds of hay fever, but most only one.

For many years hay fever sufferers received little sympathy and much ridicule from nonsufferers who simply could not understand why that which did not bother them should trouble someone else. At first there were absolutely no remedies available. Except for escape, nothing could be done but to grin and bear it. Those who could afford it ran away to areas where there was little or no hay fever. Some took a long ocean voyage. Pollen does not exist in significant quantities in the air over the sea more than a hundred miles or so from shore, becoming too widely diffused to affect the allergic. In the summer and autumn of 1937 the late Dr. E. E. Free, a prominent scientific consultant who was a lifelong hay fever sufferer, solved his problem in a novel way. He engaged a suite on one of the New York–to–Bermuda ocean liners and spent the hay fever season shuttling between the two places. He took along his secretary, files, and equipment and worked on board ship and in Bermuda (where there is no hay fever), holding consultations with clients while the ship was docked in New York. The publicity he received stimulated enough additional business to defray the expense.

The earliest hay fever remedies were mere palliatives and completely ineffective. There were such items, for example, as mentholated cigarettes and menthol inhalers. There was even a device which one inserted in the nostrils, supposedly to filter out the offending pollen. Most victims could not endure the discomfort, aside from which the contrivance was not always successful since many pollens were too small to be filtered out.

Seasonal Rhinitis, unfortunately, is not the only type of hay fever. There are other allergic disorders having similar unpleasant symptoms which are caused by an almost infinite variety of substances. Some of the most common are fungus spores; the dander of horses, dogs, cats, and other animals; feathers, wheat, and other flours; industrial dusts; house dust; orris root (used in the manufacture of face powder); flaxseed and karaya gum (used in some wave set preparations); kapok, the silklike covering of the seeds of a West and East Indian tree related to the cotton plant, which is widely used to stuff cushions and pillows; and insect scales. But this formidable list does not exhaust the substances to which people are sometimes allergic.

Those substances are all inhalants, things we inhale with the air we breathe. There are other allergens which are ingestants, things we absorb from the alimentary tract when we eat and drink. Frank A. Simon, a leading authority on allergy, says that "practically any food may act as an allergen." [3] He lists milk, eggs, wheat, tomatoes, spinach, peas, fish, and peanuts. Many drugs are also allergens, as well as some flavoring and preservative materials, and even tooth pastes and mouthwashes!

There are still other allergens which we absorb through our skins. The most common is poison ivy. There are also poison oak, sumac, primrose, and many others that are fairly common. Many drugs, chemicals, and dyes are allergens. It is probable that the length of the list of allergens is limited only by what so far has been observed and recorded.

Both the term, "allergy," and its concept are relatively new. The expression was first used in 1906 by von Pirquet, who felt the need of a new word, not otherwise used, that would "designate the altered condition which an organism achieves after acquaintance [he used the German word *Bekanntschaft*] with any organic, living, or inanimate poison." For example, an individual who previously has been injected with a serum reacts differently to it than someone who has contact with the given serum for the first time. "He is, nevertheless, as yet far from being immune because of this. All that we can say about him is that his capacity to react has been altered. I

[74]

suggest the word 'allergy' to designate this general concept of altered reactivity." [4] At first the word was used only to designate a *decreased* reactivity, though the idea of *increased reactivity* was not ruled out, certainly not by von Pirquet. When we use the term today, we refer to the *increased* reactivity that is typical of the allergic after he once has been exposed to some foreign substance. The capacity of the individual to react is acquired as the result of exposure to the same specific substance.

Once this concept was established it was possible to develop a form of treatment called hyposensitization. This is the process of making the patient progressively less sensitive to the one or more afflicting allergens by a series of increasingly concentrated subcutaneous injections of those very substances. It was first necessary, of course, to determine which allergens (usually there was more than one) were causing the trouble. The patient was given the skin test. There were several techniques, one of which was to scratch or abrade the skin without drawing blood, and then to rub the spots with those allergens that seemed most likely to be the culprits. Another was to hold the suspects in close contact with the unabraded skin for several hours by means of adhesive tape. Frequently it was necessary to test many allergens before the right ones were found. And even then the results were not certain. Such an authority as Simon admits that "many positive skin reactions are of no clinical importance. Furthermore, a negative skin reaction to a certain substance does not prove that the patient is not *clinically sensitive* to that substance." [5]

As we moved forward toward the era of the so-called "miracle drugs," one drug after another was hailed as the long-sought panacea for the allergy victim, only to be later found wanting in one way or another. First came the vasostrictors such as *ephedrine* and *benzedrine*. During World War II *benadryl* acquired considerable popularity. It provided temporary relief, frequently at the cost of dizziness and

[75]

chronic drowsiness. Another drug which some found more satisfactory was *pyribenzamine* (PBZ). The most recent on the scene were the other antihistamines.

All of these remedies provided some degree of relief for some patients. None was effective for all. In spite of them the best remedy was still an ocean voyage or a trip to some locality not subject to the menace. The next best was the complete air conditioning of one's home and office. Both of these remedies had the defect in that only the rich could afford them.

We speak with the voice of experience, for one of the authors (A. W. Pezet) has had hay fever since early childhood and has tried everything at least once. During the past year the other half of this collaboration (E. M. Abrahamson) treated him for hyperinsulinism and for the first time in forty-six years, except for years spent in California, Mexico, South America, and other immune places, he was without a single day of hay fever. This seeming miracle is no isolated coincidence, as will be seen presently.

Even if they have failed to discover the cause, the allergists have learned many interesting facts about the allergies during the past twenty-five years. They have learned that there is a hereditary predisposition toward allergies as a type of malady. Allergies run in families, different members of which may develop different allergies, more than one each, or none at all. Another curious fact which makes the allergies almost unique is that they are pre-eminently the diseases of those of relatively higher intelligence. There is a definite correlation between the hypersensitivity to allergens and intelligence: the lower animals, for example, do not have allergies. Study of these diseases undoubtedly has been retarded by our inability to use dogs and cats and rabbits for experimental purposes.

This strange correlation has led the psychoanalysts to the hypothesis that the causes of allergies are purely mental. Many allergists, in fact, sorely baffled by what one of their

[76]

number has called the "strange malady," [6] "have long suspected that deep-seated emotional disturbances lie behind
a vast number of the cases that come before them." [7] Recently,
Dr. Hyman Miller, associate clinical professor of medicine at
the University of Southern California Medical School, and
his wife and research partner, Dr. Dorothy Baruch, a well-
known Beverly Hills psychotherapist, have reported on a joint
research they are conducting. They have attempted to make
a "scientific measurement of the relationship between specific
emotional disturbances and allergies." At this incomplete
stage of their work the Millers "have found that the vast
majority of the allergic children who were brought before
them had a deeply troubled relationship with their parents—
with their mothers especially." In most of the cases there was
"maternal rejection"—that is, a mother "whose behavior toward the child is such that she *consciously or unconsciously*
has a desire to be free of the child and considers it a burden."

At this point we were reminded of the delightful Myerson
anecdote. At a meeting he attended, some psychiatrist advanced the hypothesis that epileptics are men who hate their
fathers. Myerson commented that he knew a lot of epileptic
cats who had never met their fathers. [8] In this age of the split
atom and the flying saucer, however, it is inadvisable to scoff
at anything. The Millers do not claim that all allergic children
are rejected by their mothers, nor that all rejected children
develop allergies. They do claim, however, that 98.4 per cent
of the allergic children tested were also rejected children.
"Maternal rejection," say the Millers, "is not only an almost
universal experience in the lives of allergic children, but they
differ in this respect from other groups of problem children." [9]
While the assumptions of the Millers may not be correct, the
data on which they are based have a most important bearing
on the causation of the allergies, as we shall discuss in greater
detail later.

Needless to say, the allergists as a body have ignored the

claims of maternal rejection as a causative factor in allergies. The medical profession, like other segments of humanity, is composed of a minority who believe in anything that is new and a majority who refuse to believe in anything that is new. Between them, the open-minded man of science, willing to pick up crumbs from the right and the left but unwilling to put them in his mouth until he has thoroughly tested them, has a difficult time of it.

During the past quarter century many allergists have interested themselves in blood sugar. Several investigators subjected many asthmatics to the standard diabetic two-hour Glucose Tolerance Test. They found a tendency to low fasting blood sugar levels and, when the patient drank the glucose solution for the test, the rise in blood sugar was less than in normal persons. As far as diabetes is concerned, asthmatics are even more "normal" than healthy people.[10] These observations have been known for many years, but no explanation was offered.

A word about asthma. It is an allergy identical to hay fever in almost every respect except one. It is caused by the same pollens, spores, danders, and dusts, and like hay fever it may be seasonal or perennial. It is affected by location and climate, and heredity is a causative factor. It is probably as common and as widely distributed as hay fever. It differs from hay fever in being more serious because the allergens affect the bronchi (the smaller air passages) instead of the upper portions of the respiratory tract and the conjunctivae (the pink membranes surrounding the eye). Asthma was first described in the second century by Aretaeus the Cappadocian, the same sage who gave us our first detailed description of diabetes. Though known for all these centuries, asthma has remained one of the mysterious diseases that is little understood and for which no effective cure has been devised.

If low blood sugar is characteristic of asthma, we should expect asthma to be nonexistent in diabetics whose blood sugar is high. Geneticists found that the two conditions often shared a common heredity but apparently were mutually exclusive. They very often occurred in members of the same family, but only extremely rarely in the same individual. It was thought that some defect occurred in the same hereditary factor which could take either of two directions, giving rise to diabetes OR asthma.[11]

If there is no relation between the diseases, we should expect that the percentage of diabetics with asthma should be about the same as the percentage of nondiabetics with asthma. Many observers have noticed the contrary, that either disease seems to protect its victim from the other.[12] Joslin, the great authority on diabetes, had a few patients who had suffered from asthma but lost it when they acquired diabetes.

Asthma frequently is associated with underactivity of the thyroid gland, and many asthmatics have been helped by taking thyroid extract.[13] One patient, a woman, had very severe asthmatic attacks. After a number of years of great discomfort she noticed that the attacks became progressively less severe and less frequent, finally ceasing altogether. Soon thereafter she lost a great deal of weight. She became extremely nervous and developed an unbearable palpitation of the heart. These are symptoms of toxic goiter. A basal metabolic rate determination confirmed her physician's diagnosis. The enlarged and overactive thyroid gland had to be removed. After the operation her symptoms disappeared, but the asthma, which had not troubled her for several years, returned.

A severe case of asthma, then, was arrested by a toxic goiter, an ailment which has long been known to make diabetes much more severe.

A few years ago a relationship was discovered between asthma and the amount of potassium in the blood. Asthmatics tend to have the element in excessive amounts.[14] (A treatment was devised based on this finding, but it did not prove practicable.) By contrast the serum potassium of diabetics tends to be low.

The same investigator noticed that asthmatics suffered much more when they ate excessive amounts of table salt. On the other hand, it was found that diabetics could get along with less insulin if they were given large amounts of table salt. The salt, however, had to be taken by a tube that passed through the mouth and stomach into the intestine, because such a large amount of salt was irritating to the stomach. This was not proposed as a treatment for diabetes. Obviously the needle is far less annoying than the stomach tube. But the experiment was performed on volunteers to increase our understanding of the mechanism of diabetes.[15]

All of these considerations point to a reciprocal relationship between asthma and diabetes. To tabulate:

	DIABETES	ASTHMA
Blood sugar:	*High*	*Low*
Blood potassium:	*Low*	*High*
Effect of goiter:	*Makes worse*	*Makes better*
Effect of salt:	*Makes better*	*Makes worse*

It seemed fairly well established that asthma and diabetes were opposites. Diabetes is hypoinsulinism and the physiological opposite of that is hyperinsulinism. Purely as a working hypothesis, therefore, it seemed logical to assume that asthmatics actually have hyperinsulinism. Naturally that condition would be in a mild form or asthmatics would have the typical symptoms of hyperinsulinism—hunger, fatigue, and so forth. If this assumption were correct, the patients tested should not indicate it merely statistically. It would not suffice for a majority—even a very large majority—of asthmatics to have hyperinsulinism. All asthmatics must have it. A single negative finding would be sufficient to demolish the reasoning.

Twelve consecutive, unselected patients were treated with

Seale Harris' six-hour Glucose Tolerance Test.[16] All of them produced curves which showed a late drop in blood sugar and met all of Dr. Harris' criteria for hyperinsulinism. (Subsequently these results have been repeated in several hundred cases.)

We therefore can say that asthmatics have hyperinsulinism. But, of course, not all cases of hyperinsulinism have asthmatic symptoms. In the language of the mathematician, we can say that hyperinsulinism is a necessary but not sufficient condition for the appearance of asthma.[17]

These twelve tested patients were then placed on Harris' diet. All of them improved considerably. Only two had attacks of asthma after being placed on the diet. The twelve were not so fortunate with other symptoms of allergy, such as sneezing and running of the eyes and nose. The gratifying response of these twelve patients to the dietary treatment is further evidence that hyperinsulinism has something to do with asthma. We cannot say that it is the cause of asthma. We *can* say that given the allergic sensitivity, hyperinsulinism apparently permits, if not induces, the spasm of the bronchi that produces the asthmatic attack. This is borne out by several other facts.

It has long been known that asthmatics have reason to dread the night, for "the beginning [of an attack] is said to be most frequent during the night, when the patient has had his first sleep; for instance, at two or three in the morning he suddenly wakes with a stuffy feeling in his chest, and within a short time he is in the throes of an attack of asthma." [18] If pollen were the only factor, asthmatic attacks should be more common in the daytime when flowers are open and discharging their pollen into the air. Yet, these nocturnal attacks are not fortuitous. The blood sugar in persons with hyperinsulinism reaches its minimal value at precisely those hours. During the day meals are usually frequent enough to prevent a decided fall in blood sugar in persons with *mild* hyperinsulinism.

[81]

Since the last meal is usually eaten between six and eight in the evening, there is ample time during the night for the blood sugar to drop below the normal physiological minimum.

The hyperinsulinism hypothesis also explains why intravenous injections of glucose, which are sometimes used to stop severe attacks of asthma,[19] do not succeed permanently. The rise in blood sugar will relieve the spasm, but the sudden increase in the concentration of sugar stimulates the islands of Langerhans to secrete insulin, and their overgenerous action lowers the blood sugar even below the level from which the injection of glucose first raised it. The patient then has another attack. Feeding sugar by mouth at frequent intervals and in large amounts has been recommended as a treatment for asthmatic children.[20] It has the same objection as the treatment which was at first given to the luckless patient in Chapter One. It will relieve an attack of asthma just as it relieved that patient's tachycardia, only to bring on another attack. The patient has to take the sugar with increasing frequency to ward off the attacks. On the other hand, a "ketogenic" diet—a high fat diet—has been used with considerable success in treating asthmatic children.[21] The Harris hyperinsulinism diet is ketogenic.

It seems more than merely coincidental that the drugs commonly used for the relief of asthmatic attacks, such as morphine,[22] amytal,[23] ephedrine,[24] and adrenalin,[25] all raise the blood sugar level.

Thus, our assumption that hyperinsulinism is an underlying condition in asthma seems to be confirmed by the conjunction of many factors all pointing in the same direction. If our assumption is true there should be no asthma in diabetics. Unfortunately, such combinations of apparently mutually exclusive conditions do occur, albeit very rarely. In an experience with many thousands of diabetics, only six were found who also had asthma. But six is enough to demolish the hypothesis. Unless we can find some completely valid explanation to

[82]

reconcile these six fatal discrepancies, the entire theory will have to be jettisoned.

In 1935 a woman of thirty-six, who had just had a baby, was referred for treatment by her obstetrician. Diabetes had been discovered during the last few weeks of her pregnancy. The case was relatively mild and was easily controlled by diet and small doses of insulin. She was an intelligent, co-operative patient. Her insulin dosage could be diminished as her condition improved. By the summer of 1937 she could dispense with insulin.

She was met next in a hospital in April, 1938. She had caught a cold during the previous winter and had been unable to throw it off. She had begun to have asthmatic attacks. They became increasingly frequent and severe. At the same time her diabetes took a turn for the worse. She had to resume insulin injections. By the time she came to the hospital she had respiratory difficulty most of the time and daily asthmatic attacks lasting many hours. Her nights were particularly difficult. She could only sleep sitting up.

At the hospital her condition became worse. Every test that had even the remotest connection with her condition was performed. Nothing was found. A mixture of drugs was finally discovered that would relieve the bronchial spasm and enable her to get a little sleep.

After her discharge she continued to come to the hospital—to the diabetes clinic for that ailment and to the allergy clinic for her asthma. By the fall of 1938 she was so badly off that she had to take an injection of adrenalin about every three hours. She took one before trying to sleep at night and she set a loaded hypodermic syringe on her night table. When awakened by an asthmatic attack, she would take an injection of adrenalin and the resultant relief would enable her to sleep for a while. She never got through the night without at least one such injection; frequently she had to have two. She carried a sterile syringe with her at all times. During the day,

[83]

whenever her breathing became too labored, she would step into a telephone booth to give herself an injection of adrenalin.

On November 12, 1939, she was given the six-hour Glucose Tolerance Test. The results were so startling that we include the graph of her test here:

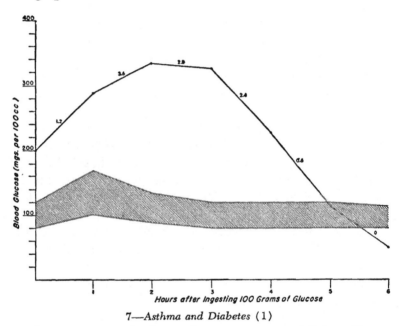

7—*Asthma and Diabetes* (1)

This curve accounts for the simultaneous occurrence of diabetes (hypoinsulinism) and asthma (which we believe to be accompanied by hyperinsulinism).

She had promised not to take any adrenalin during the night before her test. It will be remembered that adrenalin causes the liver to discharge some of its glycogen into the blood in the form of soluble glucose. But she had found it urgently necessary to take an injection of adrenalin in order to be able to breathe. She was wheezing slightly when she came in for the test. Her fasting blood sugar was compara-

[84]

tively low for her, only 200. The normal fasting blood sugar range, of course, is between 80 and 120. Her wheeze disappeared a few minutes after she was given the drink containing the 100 grams of glucose. An hour later her blood sugar was 238. The sugar level was then followed by taking samples of blood at hourly intervals and analyzing them for sugar. When the drop occurred, the wheeze returned. Finally her blood sugar level dropped below the normal range and the test had to be stopped by giving her some food.

If the test had been conducted for only two hours, it would have revealed diabetes. Such a case of simultaneous diabetes and asthma would have destroyed our hypothesis. There had been an abnormally large rise, however, and the level did not reach the initial value in two hours. These are indications of diabetes. By prolonging the period of investigation, it was seen that the rise was followed by a dip into the abnormally low range characteristic of hyperinsulinism. This combination, or alternation of high and low, is what Harris called *dysinsulinism*. It will be remembered that Harris attributed this condition to some delay in the production of insulin so that once released it is secreted too liberally. This enables the patient to have alternating periods of abnormally high and abnormally low blood sugar levels, or diabetes and hyperinsulinism. This discovery removed the only objection to our theory. We now have a complete explanation of why it is possible for the patient to have both diabetes and asthma. Her treatment previous to this discovery had, of course, been a little ridiculous. She had been taking insulin for her diabetes, thus lowering her blood sugar and making her asthma worse. When she then took adrenalin for her asthma, she raised her blood sugar level and made her diabetes worse. The repeated injections of the two drugs made both conditions worse and necessitated steadily increased doses of both drugs. A vicious cycle with a vengeance!

The discovery led to a rational treatment for her antagonistic conditions. She was taken off both drugs and given the Harris diet. Of course, the interdiction of adrenalin was not sudden—she could not sweat out her cure, she had to breathe. But she soon found that she could get along with progressively less adrenalin. She finally was able to abandon its use entirely. Her diabetes was very mild and she passed under 10 grams of sugar daily, meeting our criterion for good control. In effect, we permitted the asthma and diabetes to neutralize each other.

For a while the patient followed her dietary instructions religiously, but then she slipped and drank coffee. After a few weeks the wheeze returned. She had the good sense to give up coffee for good, and the wheeze disappeared again, never to return.

This patient was brought before a medical group. A famous allergist was in the audience. In his discussion he claimed that the treatment was not scientific because "it was assumed that the patient had hyperinsulinism." It was impossible to convince him that the assumption was a working hypothesis that was completely justified by the results. He talked of allergens, the various substances capable of inducing allergies. He also spoke of atopens, which are nothing more than a more limited type of allergen. ("By atopy," wrote Coca, who introduced the term, "is meant certain clinical forms of human hypersensitivity that do not occur, so far as is known, in the lower animals, and which are subject to hereditary influence. In this category have been included thus far only asthma and hay fever, but it is generally thought that eczema and certain forms of drug and food idiosyncrasy will eventually be placed with these." In other words an atopen is an allergen restricted to the commonest forms of allergy! Unfortunately, medical science is full of such words which have their specific uses but which are too often used as a smoke screen.

The patient had been treated in this allergist's clinic. She was asked how much adrenalin she took while under his care. She replied that she had required six or seven injections daily. The allergist still was not convinced even after she had told him that since being treated for her dysinsulinism she had not needed adrenalin for six months! Such is the tyranny of routinized thinking even in an outstanding specialist. Is it any wonder that the rank and file of the medical profession are slow to adopt a revolutionary change?

Another patient with both asthma and diabetes had an almost identical experience. Although this patient drank coffee

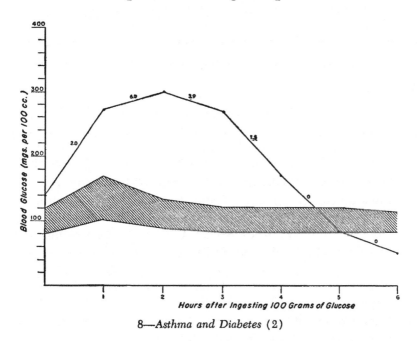

8—*Asthma and Diabetes* (2)

on occasion, she was sufficiently faithful to her diet not to require any adrenalin. She received a postcard from the allergy clinic asking why she had neglected treatment for so many months. Her chart had the interesting notation written in the allergy clinic: "Sleeps on a feather pillow, contrary to advice!" (The exclamation point was on the original notation from

[87]

which this was quoted.) The same chart contained a notation written in the diabetes clinic. It read: "BUT SHE HAS NO ASTHMATIC ATTACKS!!!"

Several other patients were investigated in the same fashion. They all followed the same pattern.[26]

This success led to the investigation of that other common allergic condition—hay fever. Hay fever patients tested exhibited the same type of hyperinsulinism sugar tolerance curve. They were helped considerably by the diet, but they still experienced morning sneezes (when the blood sugar is low). Their eye symptoms were not relieved much.[27] This was a puzzle for many years. Now, however, we can arrest hay fever too merely by adding calcium to the treatment.

Rheumatic fever, which has been known since the sixteenth century, is one of the most devastating diseases of childhood. It has been estimated that more than 10 per cent of the deaths occurring before the age of eight are due to acute rheumatic fever and its sequelae (the diseased condition that follows a disease). There must be close to two hundred thousand cases a year in the United States, and at least one million Americans now bear the marks of rheumatic infections suffered in childhood. Rheumatic fever is not a "reportable disease," so that these figures are only estimates, but they are conservative estimates. Everyone who has suffered from rheumatic fever sustains some damage to his heart. This may be slight, manifesting itself only many years later, or very severe, leading to a badly damaged circulation. Over 25 per cent of all cardiac deaths (which lead all others and now number close to four hundred fifty thousand a year) are due to rheumatic fever. Compared with this dread killer and maimer, poliomyelitis fades into insignificance. Why, one might ask, is so much more public attention accorded to infantile paralysis than to rheumatic fever? We believe it is because of the visual impressionability of the public. Polio cripples visibly, while the damage done by rheumatic fever is not so obvious to the naked eye.

Although rheumatic fever very frequently follows an upper respiratory infection, such as an attack of tonsilitis, no infective agent has been proved to be its cause. There is apparently some hereditary predisposition to rheumatic fever, for it is rather common in some families. A certain physical type seems more susceptible to it than others—the fair-haired, blue-eyed, light-skinned type with a tendency to freckle. Environment plays an important part too, for it is most frequent in cold, damp climates and during the cold, damp months. It has been called "acute" rheumatic fever, but that is a misnomer, for the cases never really come to an end. Patients are subject to periodic "exacerbations"—repeated outbreaks—when the smoldering fire bursts into flame.

There is a great deal of evidence to support the view that rheumatic fever is an allergic reaction to a focus of infection in the tonsils. Some of the skin manifestations (*erythema multiforme* and *erythema nodosa*) resemble hives (*urticaria*) and the rashes produced by allergy to inoculations.[28] Since hyperinsulinism is an attendant condition in other forms of allergy, the question naturally arises: is it also in rheumatic fever? In answer to this, there is the supporting evidence that diabetics seldom show signs of rheumatic heart disease.[29] Against this is the understanding that diabetes is usually a disease of late adult life whereas rheumatic fever rarely occurs after childhood. But the latter statement is true only of the initial attack of rheumatic fever. Not all children succumb, and most of them reach adult life. Consequently, unless there is some antagonism between the two diseases, there is no reason why adults who had rheumatic fever in childhood should not acquire diabetes in about the same ratio as the general population.

Several patients who had recently recovered from attacks of rheumatic fever were subjected to the same hyperinsulinism investigations that had proved fruitful with other types of allergics. The results completely vindicated our theory.[30] Patients treated with the Harris diet went through two winters without a single exacerbation, although most of them had a sore throat or two during each cold season.

This experiment was followed by the examination of a group of "inactive" cases—persons who had not had any *recent* attacks. It was found that these people could be divided into two groups. The first group had had several exacerbations. The Glucose Tolerance Test showed that all the persons in this group had hyperinsulinism. After following the diet for a while, they were able to report that they had had no more attacks of rheumatic fever in spite of episodes of sore throat. The second group of persons had had only one attack of rheumatic fever and that many years before. The persons in this group did not show a drop in blood sugar following the ingestion of the glucose solution. They did not have hyperinsulinism. Their dietary history was gone into in detail. It was learned that these people never drank coffee and that they didn't care for sweets. In other words, their long habit of doing without the exciting causes of hyperinsulinism had removed that factor which is apparently necessary for the development of allergy to the infection in their throats.

It is interesting that this work was confirmed before it was performed. Coburn and Moore, who had been working on the problem of rheumatic fever for many years, reported that all of the patients they investigated had been eating too little protein. All other factors, including minerals and vitamins, were entirely adequate. They put their patients on a diet with more protein food. Simultaneously, of course, they had to cut down on the carbohydrates to prevent fattening them. After going on this diet, none of them had any rheumatic attacks, although they continued to have sore throats. In effect, they had given their patients much of the Conn diet, which also eliminates hyperinsulinism.[31]

The diet of the poor is usually heavy in such foods as bread, spaghetti, and especially potatoes—all carbohydrates—because they are relatively cheap. The preponderant incidence of rheumatic fever in the slums is well known. A team of English investigators noticed and commented upon this dietary imbalance among rheumatics. They gave the children under their care more liberal quantities of milk and cream. There was no significant reduction in the number of their attacks of sore throat, but the rheumatic attacks dropped to one third of what they had been.[32]

Unfortunately, neither of these groups of investigators used the Glucose Tolerance Test. Nevertheless, it would appear reasonably well established that the changes in diet were related to lessening their patients' susceptibility to rheumatic fever attacks. Both groups used measures that tend to diminish insulin secretion. Their success was only partial because they did not complete treatment with the Harris regimen.

This conception of the hyperinsulinism factor in rheumatic fever was also confirmed by animal experimentation. It had never been possible to produce the lesions of rheumatic fever in animals. Foci of infection with those organisms that had been suspect of producing rheumatic fever in humans had created only local abscesses, generalized blood stream infections, and so forth. They did not produce rheumatic lesions, say, in the heart, which autopsy has shown in man. Schultz produced such abscesses in rabbits and then administered insulin to them daily. When he had reduced their blood sugar by an excess of insulin, these infected animals showed lesions resembling those of human rheumatic fever.[33]

Of course, not all cases of rheumatic fever occur in the slums. Why do the children of more affluent parents get the disease? It is easily demonstrated that well-to-do rheumatic children are finicky eaters. They eat large amounts of sweets, which their more fortunately situated parents can afford. The parents usually are so happy to have these children eat

[91]

anything at all that they gladly indulge their dietary whims.

The theory seems to be justified that there are several factors necessary to the development of rheumatic fever. First, there must be a focus of infection. Second, there must be an inherent allergic susceptibility which, third, by improper diet is fully developed. The combination of all three factors is necessary to produce rheumatic fever. The final piece of evidence offered in support of this view is the fact that rheumatic persons are susceptible to and often acquire one or more of the other allergies. The evidence is in the record of innumerable case histories.

Another disease which, like asthma, hay fever, and rheumatic fever, only rarely occurs simultaneously with diabetes is peptic ulcer. This is fortunate, indeed, because it would be difficult to devise a diet to care for both conditions. In ulcer we feed the patient large amounts of fat, a food which we avoid in the modern treatment of diabetes.[34] On the other hand, a high intake of carbohydrate is of benefit in diabetes because it tends to keep the blood sugar level lower. Such starches are avoided in cases of ulcer.

There are many statistical studies that confirm the widely held opinion that the two conditions only rarely occur together.[35] Joslin believes that this can be explained by the difference in the ages at which people usually have the two conditions.[36] Ulcer is a disease of early adult life, diabetes of later occurrence. We do not believe that this satisfactorily explains the fact. In the first place, once acquired in early adult life, ulcers tend to become chronic. While they are not cured, one does not die of them. One learns to live with them. This is corroborated by the low death rate from ulcers—only 5.8 per 100,000—against 24.8 for diabetics, in spite of all that can be done for them. Consequently, we should expect the majority of ulcer patients to survive to the diabetic age. Furthermore, unless there is some other factor working to pre-

[92]

vent it, the high fat diet given to ulcer patients should pre-
dispose them to the later acquisition of diabetes.[37] Yet no
evidence has ever been submitted to indicate any particularly
high incidence of diabetes among treated ulcer patients.

It has been generally recognized by the medical profession
that ulcers and gall bladder disease tend to occur in two
distinct constitutional types which differ sharply in many
respects.[38] This gall bladder type is very frequently diabetic.
Unless all our ideas about constitution and disease are wrong,
we should expect the opposite type to be relatively free from
diabetes. That the restriction of fats helps to keep gall bladder
patients freer of symptoms also suggests that gall bladder
disease and diabetes attack similar constitutional types.

But no matter what the true explanation may be, experience in most diabetes clinics will show that very few of their
patients have peptic ulcer. (This discussion demonstrates the
difficulty in drawing valid conclusions from statistical analyses. The complexity of biological phenomena leads us to make
simplifying assumptions in order to reduce the number of
variables. We can thus bring the problem within the limited
powers of human reasoning. But we are actually bending the
solution to our mind's desire. Too often we have begged the
question.)

Harris has shown that among the many symptomatic disguises assumed by hyperinsulinism are those of peptic ulcer.[39]
Even a moderately low blood sugar level may induce the
rapid and frequent constrictions of the stomach after meals
that is characteristic of peptic ulcer.[40] There is, indeed, good
reason to believe that these spasms which simulate those of
organic lesions in the stomach and duodenum may actually
be the precursors of the development of ulcers.

The assumption that peptic ulcer, like asthma, hay fever,
and rheumatic fever, is associated with hyperinsulinism was
subjected to direct experimental verification. To avoid the
pitfalls of reasoning from statistics, it was made a condition

[93]

of the experiment that a single disagreement would demolish the hypothesis. A group of sixteen persons with symptoms of peptic ulcer were submitted to the six-hour Glucose Tolerance Test.[41] All had the classical signs and symptoms of peptic ulcer—heartburn and pain related to meals and relieved by alkalies; seasonal variation; and abdominal tenderness. None had received any dietary treatment. Those who had any marked arteriosclerosis were rejected, because this condition might mimic true peptic ulcer. Similarly, ulcer cases with complications such as blood in the stool, vomiting of blood, or perforation were excluded. In each case the diagnosis of peptic ulcer was as certain as any clinical diagnosis can be. The cases were divided into three groups on the basis of the X-ray findings: gastric ulcers, duodenal ulcers, and those in which the X ray failed to demonstrate any anatomical lesion, or at least any large enough to be seen. The results are tabulated below:

Case	Fasting	Mg. glucose per 100 cc. of blood at 1–6 hrs. after ingesting 100 grams of glucose					
		1 hr.	2 hr.	3 hr.	4 hr.	5 hr.	6 hr.
I. GASTRIC ULCER							
1	98	162	110	93	88	72	60
2	65	127	86	86	82	57*	
3	87	134	100	78	66	63	67
4	110	138	148	80	57	62	66
5	78	130	84	75	75	70	52
II. DUODENAL ULCER							
6	66	118	125	80	72	60	55
7	87	142	96	80	66*		
8	88	136	82	81	82	76	57
9	88	126	102	90	72	63	58
10	76	133	74	60	56*		
11	112	142	110	66	58	60	60
12	108	146	100	76	60†		

[94]

		1 hr.	2 hr.	3 hr.	4 hr.	5 hr.	6 hr.
		III. NO X-RAY FINDINGS					
13	96	144	100	72	71	55*	
14	86	124	80	77	76	72	61
15	84	136	82	70	63	62	53
16	102	145	98	92	84	66	61

* Test had to be stopped because of severe pain.
† Test had to be stopped 20 minutes before the hour because of pain.

These results are conclusive. They show the futility of placing any dependence on the extremely variable fasting blood sugar level. They show further that the so-called "flatness" of the curve is a poor indication of increased sugar tolerance. Whereas many of these cases show a relatively high jump on the first hour, only one, No. 4 is above 140 at the second hour, and that by a very slight amount, but by the fourth hour most and by the fifth hour all have begun to dip into the hypoglycemic range. These uniformly low values confirmed the prediction that all cases of peptic ulcer would have hyperinsulinism.

There remains one important question. As with asthma and rheumatic fever, we must explain the rare cases in which a patient has both diabetes and peptic ulcer. If not, our hypothesis must be abandoned. Only three such cases were available for investigation. All three happened to have duodenal ulcer. They were given the six-hour Glucose Tolerance Test. The results are tabulated below:

Case	Fasting		Mg. per 100 cc. after 1–6 hrs.					
		1 hr.	2 hr.	3 hr.	4 hr.	5 hr.	6 hr.
17	118	186	144	100	75	66	66
18	98	166	222	124	82	60	57
19	100	232	188	102	90	78	64

Again the curves are typical of what Seale Harris called

[95]

*dys*insulinism. The first portion of each is typically diabetic. Then they topple into the low blood sugar range in the precipitous manner that proclaims the strange dysinsulinism condition.

All of these peptic ulcer patients were treated with the Harris diet for hyperinsulinism. The patients did quite well on it. None of them had to take alkalies for longer than a few weeks, while many of them did not require any at all. The dysinsulinism patients were treated exactly like the others, since their diabetes was mild enough to be ignored. It is an interesting coincidence that the modified Sippy diet widely used in the ambulatory treatment of peptic ulcer greatly resembles the Harris hyperinsulinism diet. We find that the prohibition of coffee, which is a part not only of the Sippy but of all ulcer regimens, on purely empirical grounds, is now seen to have a rational, scientific basis.

It must be mentioned that none of these cases of peptic ulcer, as with the cases of asthma, hay fever, and rheumatic fever that were studied, exhibited any of the *major* symptoms of hyperinsulinism such as ravenous hunger, acute fatigue, sweating, or palpitation. These symptoms are to be found only in marked cases of the disease. But a moderate hyperinsulinism that accompanies other conditions and can be revealed only by the six-hour Glucose Tolerance Test would seem, as a result of these investigations, to be fairly common.

We cannot say positively that hyperinsulinism precedes an ulcer and is causally related to it, but there is some justification for believing that such is the case. Several cases were investigated which differed from known cases of anatomical peptic ulcer only in the absence of positive X-ray findings. According to all the symptoms they were otherwise peptic ulcer cases. They had the same typical curves for their Glucose Tolerance Tests. They responded to the identical dietary treatment. They were in every way ulcer cases except that no visible ulcer could be seen on the X-ray plate. This is signifi-

[96]

cant, something that future investigations should clear up.

So far we have presented *facts* which have been verified by scientific experimentation with unanimous—not merely statistically promising—results. Consequently, a bit of speculation would not now seem unjustified.

It has been shown that hyperinsulinism has been found to be a condition necessary to the development of such diversified diseases as ulcer, asthma, and rheumatic fever. All of these conditions are markedly constitutional diseases. The protean nature of hyperinsulinism becomes understandable when we consider the effect of chronic low blood sugar. The normal level of blood sugar is *not* the 80 to 120 mg. per 100 cc. of blood given in the medical books. That is the normal *fasting* level, and fasting is not a normal condition. It produces the unpleasant sensation of hunger which leads to its prompt relief. The really *normal* blood sugar level during the waking, working, and eating hours of the day fluctuates about a mean of 140 mg. per 100 cc. In hyperinsulinism this level is considerably lower and we have, in effect, a state of chronic partial blood sugar starvation. But sugar in the form of glucose is used to nourish all the cells of the body. Their health requires an adequate amount of glucose at all times. If inadequate nourishment is long continued we can expect some weak spot to break down sooner or later. We cannot predict where the break will occur, just as we cannot be certain where the automobile persistently running on too lean a mixture will give trouble.

During World War II an X-ray specialist was in charge of the X-ray department at the post hospital of a large army camp. He made rather frequent diagnoses of peptic ulcer, which angered his commanding general. Unknown to the specialist, the general sent a number of the X-ray plates to the Mayo Clinic for interpretation. The diagnosis of ulcer was confirmed in each case.

It was noticed that the incidence of peptic ulcer among

servicemen was much greater than it had been in World War I. Psychosomatic medicine was now in great vogue. It was held that the increase was due to the greater difficulty in adjustment to military life. We do not believe that the difficulty of adjustment in the training camps was any more severe than in World War I. Certainly if such a thing were a cause for ulcers, there was a much greater cause in the combat divisions, where men were shooting with live bullets and not merely practicing. But the incidence of ulcer among the combat divisions was much less than in the training camps. In the light of the revelations we have made, there is a simple explanation for this supposed phenomenon. Anyone ever connected in any way with military life has seen the soft drink dispensing machines in every building of all cantonments. The men coming off training maneuvers were hot and thirsty. Frequently there was no really cold water to drink; these machines with their ice-cold sweet drinks were quite handy. The men would drink several bottles at a time. Among combat troops, however, the stuff frequently was rationed at three bottles per man per week, if that. This, we believe, is why there were fewer cases of ulcer among the combat troops than in the camps, and fewer in World War I than in World War II. The men were getting less *caffeine*.

Americans are the largest consumers of coffee in the world. Not content with that excessive use of caffeine in the fine aromatic and ancient *caffa* of Abyssinia, we have concocted and popularized by stupendous high pressure advertising a host of soft drinks previously unknown to the civilized world. These sugar-laden and caffeine-containing carbonated beverages are imbibed by adult, teen-ager, and even children in an ever-increasing and staggering volume. They are without doubt having some effect upon the incidence of diseases that result from chronic partial blood sugar starvation. The matter deserves immediate serious consideration.

5

Body, *Mind,* and Sugar

RICHARD H. HOFFMANN—NEUROSES AND HYPERINSULINISM—THE MODIFIED GLU-COSE TOLERANCE TEST—THE "TAPERING OFF" DIET—MORE CASE HISTORIES—SID-NEY A. PORTIS—LIFE SITUATIONS—"FA-TIGUE"—CIGARETTES—"THE TIRED BUSI-NESSMAN"

So FAR we have been concerned with the *body,* and with *sugar* as it affects the body. Now let us turn to the *mind.*

In 1945 Dr. Richard Horace Hoffmann asked me (E. M. Abrahamson) to work with him. An eminent psychiatrist, Dr. Hoffmann had devoted his medical career to the treatment of countless "neurotics." My experience, on the other hand, had been in metabolic diseases. In the course of some twenty years I had seen several thousand diabetics, and during the previous ten years I had become acquainted with hyperin-sulinism through my research in that field. I asked Dr. Hoffmann why he wished to form such an unusual association—a psychiatrist and an internist. When I heard his answer I quickly accepted the flattering offer.

The answer? This story:

[99]

While visiting a patient in a psychiatric hospital Dr. Hoffmann was asked by a colleague to talk with a woman who refused to answer questions; she was "negativistic." Dr. Hoffmann went to the patient's room. He sniffed the air and detected a urinous odor on the patient's breath. He asked his colleague if the urea nitrogen of the blood had been determined. It had not. The patient was on the verge of uremic coma from Bright's disease. She had not answered her psychiatrist's questions because she was not completely aware of being questioned.

"That's something I don't want to happen in my office," Dr. Hoffmann told me.

Dr. Hoffmann is an excellent clinician. He believes that most neurotics are the way they are because some underlying and undiscovered bodily ailment contributes to their anxiety. Like me, he feels that the expression "psychosomatic" was poorly chosen because so many people read into it a causative relation that was not originally intended. The notion that the mind *causes* somatic disease makes the tail wag the dog.

After our association had continued a few months, we discussed the problem of blood sugar in neuroses. Dr. Hoffmann had been interested in blood chemistry in psychiatric disorders for many years. Curiously, he had but one diabetic patient. She had been "inherited" from his father who was not a psychiatrist, and she was not neurotic.

A person on whom a diagnosis of diabetes is made experiences a severe emotional shock. He realizes that he has an incurable disease—one that can only be arrested and controlled, and with which he will have to live by exercising rigorous self-denial punctuated with daily stabs of the dreaded insulin syringe. One would expect a person experiencing such an emotional shock to become highly disturbed. But the experience of practically every diabetes clinic reveals the astonishing fact that diabetics are, as a rule, very phlegmatic people. Indeed, it is usually the doctor who has to worry about their condition for them. Diabetics are notoriously uncooperative. They seem either unwilling or unable to treat their malady with its merited respect. Cajolery, explanation, and even stern warnings and threats seem inadequate to break down the cavalier attitude most diabetics display toward their illness. The diabetes specialist is repeatedly struck with the futility of even attempting scientific control of his patients, especially because diabetes is the disease par excellence in which the patient's cooperation is of the utmost importance. The death rate of 28.4 per one hundred thousand for a disease from which no one now needs to die—a rate equal to that from fatal motor vehicle accidents—attests to the appalling indifference of most diabetics.

Diabetics are singularly unaffected by many ills to which flesh is heir, and we have seen how often hyperinsulinism accompanies those conditions. It has been recognized that manifest hyperinsulinism can be accompanied by many psychic phenomena—depressive states, anxiety, and other symptoms that have been lumped together as "neuroses." [1] A masterly review in the *Oxford Looseleaf Medicine* states that "hypoglycemia [low blood sugar] as a disease entity should be kept in mind constantly by all physicians, particularly those doing neuropsychiatric work. When seen for the first time and in the absence of a good history, the attack [of low blood sugar] may suggest some brain diseases, such as infection, neoplasm [tumor], or vascular accident [apoplexy]. Because of their paroxysmal nature, the attacks may suggest epilepsy, acute alcoholism, amnesia, or some functional disorder such as hysteria. It is for these reasons that patients with hypoglycemia frequently are referred to neurological or psychiatric clinics." [2]

A group of two hundred and twenty "neurotic" patients in whom the primary complaint was a mental depression or anxiety state, revealing itself in the myriad and bizarre fantasies of the neurotic nature and disposition, were investigated from this point of view. The first cases, which had been referred for psychiatric treatment, gave indications that the psychic disturbance was overlaid with an embroidery of physical symptoms that aroused the suspicion that these neurotics also had hyperinsulinism. It is always easier to treat a psychiatric patient if any physical ailments are first corrected. So these persons were subjected to the six-hour Glucose Tolerance Test to determine the correctness of the physical diagnosis. It was found that most of these patients actually had hyperinsulinism. Before any psychiatric treatment was attempted they were put on the Harris diet. Not only did they improve with respect to their physical complaints, but their purely psychic symptoms waned and abated. They became so much more receptive to psychiatric persuasion that the mental treatment no longer had to fight against the usual resistance that neurotics display toward suggestion.

This success, obtained in cases where the physical complaints made the coexistence of hyperinsulinism seem likely, led to the assumption that hyperinsulinism, in a mild degree, might be the physical background to the portrait of the so-called neurotic in all or at least the vast majority of cases. To determine whether this might, indeed, be the case, patients who made no reference whatever to any of the classical symptoms of hyperinsulinism, such as hunger and fatigue, but who complained of all sorts of depressions, phobias, compulsions—in brief, the psychic complaints—were then subjected to the same investigation by means of the six-hour Glucose Tolerance Test. The results were amazing. Most of these patients actually had a mild hyperinsulinism. It was so mild that it could be discovered only by chemical test. The correction through proper diet of this purely metabolic condition alleviated the psychic symptoms of the persons in this group just as effectively as it had improved the condition of those who also had physical symptoms of hyperinsulinism. In other words, the psychic and somatic (physical) disturbances were the treble and base of the same discord.

The six-hour Glucose Tolerance Test is somewhat troublesome to both the patient and the laboratory. The patient must give six hours of his time to it, while the technician must make seven determinations of the blood sugar level. In order to save time, therefore, the test was modified. The patient's fasting blood sugar was first determined. Then he was given a bottle containing a 100-gram glucose solution. The patient was instructed to take it home and chill it in the refrigerator. He was to eat nothing after 8 P.M. He was to awaken at 4 A.M., drink the glucose solution flavored with lemon juice, and then go back to sleep. At 10 A.M., having had nothing else to eat or drink except water he would report to the laboratory, and a single blood sugar determination would be made. This would be sufficient to determine a diagnosis of hyperinsulinism.[3]

This, however, did not prove practicable. Many of the patients came to the laboratory in the throes of an attack of hypoglycemia (low blood sugar), while some were even too sick to make the trip. Again the test was modified. The sugar solution was taken at five instead of four in the morning, and the patient reported to the laboratory at nine-thirty instead of ten. Two blood samples were taken, at ten and eleven. This gave the fasting, fifth- and sixth-hour blood sugar levels. The patient was asleep through the first four hours of the test, when the blood sugar levels are not particularly significant for hyperinsulinism. (It is in the first two hours that diabetes would be revealed.) In manifest hyperinsulinism the drop may occur before the fifth hour after taking the glucose solution—at the fourth hour usually—but in the milder forms the drop is delayed until the fifth, and often the sixth, hour. These two hours, then, are the most significant in the determination of mild hyperinsulinism. The complete test is necessary only

[103]

when the patient is suspected of having a severer form of the condition. If the blood sugar level at 10 A.M. is below 70 milligrams per 100 cubic centimeters, the diagnosis has been confirmed, and the patient may be fed. If it does not fall below 70 milligrams, the blood sugar level is determined again at 11 A.M. If this examination does not reveal a drop, the test is abandoned. The patient does not have hyperinsulinism.

Those "neurotic" patients with hyperinsulinism were all placed on the modified Harris diet. After about a month the Glucose Tolerance Test was repeated to see if the somatic condition had subsided. It was soon discovered that this was a most undesirable procedure. The large dose of unaccustomed sugar "upset the applecart," and the patients suffered a recurrence of their original symptoms. The absence of tenderness in the left upper quadrant of the abdomen—the presence of which Harris had found to be the only *sign* of hyperinsulinism—is now a sufficient and very satisfactory indication of the return to normal. The tail of the pancreas where most of the islands of Langerhans are located becomes sensitive to pressure in hyperinsulinism. This sensitivity is a true sign, not a symptom. It can be observed objectively by the examiner, because the abdominal muscles go into spastic contraction to protect the sensitive underlying structures. When the condition of hyperinsulinism has been corrected, the tenderness and spasm are not elicited.

It was soon discovered that it was too great a shock to the body to allow the patient to discard his diet all at once. To step down gradually toward normal feeding, the diet was modified to the following.

After a few weeks on this modified diet the patient was permitted to eat a sweet dessert once a day with the heaviest meal. With continued improvement the diet was completely abandoned, except for three final instructions: the patient was to dilute his sweets with intelligence; he was to shun caffeine in all forms; and he was *always* to eat a bedtime snack.

[104]

MODIFIED HYPERINSULINISM DIET FOR
TAPERING OFF

Breakfast—Fruit or juice; cereal (dry or cooked) with
milk or cream and/or 1 egg with or without
two slices of ham or bacon; only one slice of
bread or toast with plenty of butter; beverage.

Lunch—Meat, fish, cheese or eggs; salad (large serving of lettuce, tomato, or Waldorf salad with
mayonnaise or French dressing); buttered
vegetables if desired; only one slice of bread
or toast with plenty of butter; dessert; beverage.

Midafternoon—Glass of milk.

Dinner—Soup if desired (not thickened with flour);
liberal portion of meat, fish, or poultry; vegetables; potatoes, rice, noodles, spaghetti,
and macaroni (may be eaten in moderation
only with this meal); one slice of bread if
desired; dessert or crackers and cheese; beverage.

Bedtime—Snack (milk, crackers and cheese, sandwich,
fruit, etc.).

All vegetables and fruits are permissible. Fruit may be
cooked or raw, with or without cream but without sugar.
Canned fruits should be packed without sugar.

Lettuce, mushrooms, and nuts may be taken as freely as
desired.

Juice—Any unsweetened fruit or vegetable juice except
grape juice or prune juice.

Beverages—Weak tea (tea ball, not brewed); decaffeinated
coffee; coffee substitutes. May be sweetened with saccharin.

[105]

Desserts—Fruit; unsweetened gelatin; junket (made from tablets, not from mix).

Alcoholic and soft drinks—Club soda, *dry* ginger ale, whiskies, and other DISTILLED liquors.

AVOID ABSOLUTELY—Sugar, candy, and other sweets, cake, pie, pastries, sweet custards, puddings, and ice cream. Caffeine—ordinary coffee, strong brewed tea, and other beverages containing caffeine.

Wines, cordials, cocktails, and beer.

The patients responded amazingly well to this treatment. Following are a few typical cases:

1. *T.K., male, 43 years old.* For six years he had upset his family with violent temper tantrums, invariably at mealtime. He was generally quite amiable, however, after eating. Obviously his attacks occurred when his blood sugar level was low. After a few weeks on the diet, the patient reported that the tantrums had abated and finally disappeared.

2. *B.L., female, 47 years old.* For twenty years she had suffered from claustrophobia. She refused to enter a vehicle or an elevator, and would never go out unaccompanied. After some three weeks on the diet, she found the courage to ride the subway—for the first time in her life! At first she demanded companionship, but eventually she traveled alone. Within six months she gained twenty much-needed pounds and changed from a scrawny, prematurely aged person to an alert, vigorous woman.

3. *S.I., female, 21 years old.* She was shy, diffident, introverted. Despondent over her sick mother, the girl was obsessed with the fantasy that the woman had cancer and would soon die, and that she herself would commit suicide. She suffered apprehensive nightmares from which she would awaken in a cold sweat (the result of the extreme drop in blood sugar). She brought reports from the many physicians

who had examined her, stating that she had low blood pressure, anemia, and "tissue starvation." A week after starting the diet she began to feel better and soon lost all her fears.

4. *J.P., male, 38 years old.* He was phobic and apprehensive. Both his parents had died of cancer, and he was obsessed that he too would succumb to that disease. He neglected his business to work in the cancer movement, but without relief. He became gloomy, depressed, and antisocial, and suffered chronic fatigue, headaches, and vague abdominal distress. After being on the diet for two months he returned to his work with renewed interest and ambition. (After a period of good behavior he went on a sweet spree, but was brought to his senses when his depression recurred.) By now he has forgotten his preoccupation with cancer.

5. *E.W., female, 54 years old.* This woman had a long history of depression. During the preceding 17 years she had been out socially only four times! She had consulted more than sixty doctors and had been in more than twenty sanatoria. Her last trip to a sanatorium was at the suggestion of a psychiatrist who prescribed shock treatment, but the resident physician wisely dissuaded her from it. In addition to her psychic complaints she suffered from violent menopausal symptoms. She was placed on the diet on a Tuesday. The following Saturday evening she asked her husband to take her to a motion picture for the first time in years! She has continued to improve and, except for her severe menopausal flashes, feels quite well.

This case illustrates the grave danger of the improper selection of cases for shock treatment. Shock once was considered a panacea for all psychic ills, but we now know that it is advisable only for maniacal conditions. Shock renders the depressed person inert so that he no longer burdens his family and friends with his complaints. It is fine for those who have contact with the patient—they are relieved of an irritation—but the patient himself is still further depressed. The effect of

[107]

shock on a depressed person is an exaggeration of that of a sedative and only makes his condition worse.

Usually the so-called neurotic—the individual who finds it difficult to adjust to his environment—is so engrossed with his misgivings that he is difficult to question and impress. Like light-struck photographic plates, his brain cells take dim and foggy pictures of suggestions made to him. He is "negativistic"—so self-interpretive as to be impervious to whatever reaches his mind from without. He listens more to his inner voice forming the next question *he* is going to ask, or to the next complaint *he* is going to make, than to the most sincere adjurations of the psychiatrist. His brain is ill-nourished and tired from attempting to work without adequate fuel. His fatigue has begotten apprehension and his apprehension has sired distortion. Frequently he complains of many somatic ills.

Earlier it was pointed out that while chronic partial sugar starvation of the body's cells eventually would affect some "weak spot," the location of such a spot could not be predicted. Now, however, we can qualify that statement. Since the cells of the brain are those that depend wholly upon the moment-to-moment blood sugar level for nourishment, they are perhaps the most susceptible to damage. The disturbingly large and ever-increasing number of neurotics in our population makes this clearly evident.

After restoration of the proper nutrition to the brain, these so-called neurotics rapidly became more receptive to psychiatric persuasion. It was then that they could begin to see where the shoe pinched, where the square peg had been jammed into the round hole, where, in short, they had come into conflict with many aspects of life. And soon such patients ceased to be neurotic and were able to return to contentment in profitable pursuits. We may say that these patients had suffered from hunger not only of the body but also of the mind.

[108]

When their brains were bathed in a nutrient fluid richer in sugar, they were again able to take "fortune's buffets and rewards with equal thanks." [4]

In support of these findings, Fabrykant and Pacella have reported electroencephalographic (brain wave) changes in hyperinsulinism.[5] It has also been shown that mental patients lack the ability to mobilize sugar in response to mental stress.[6] It is felt that this failure to respond normally is due to the fact that an excess of insulin smothers the action of the adrenal hormones to which it is antagonistic.

Of the two hundred and twenty patients who were first subjected to the Glucose Tolerance Test, two hundred and five were shown to have hyperinsulinism. All were successfully treated by means of the modified Harris diet (and by injections which will be described later). The treatment has been continued with almost seven hundred patients at this writing. In EVERY case in which the Glucose Tolerance Test has shown that hyperinsulinism was present—and these were more than 90 per cent of the total number—the patient lost his purely psychic symptoms within ten days of initiating the treatment. But another month or more is required to make the treatment stick. Several patients have learned by bitter experience that they must never take caffeine in any form. In fact, caffeine is so much of a causative factor in this kind of depression that the condition might be regarded as a form of caffeine poisoning. The reputed and widely accepted harmlessness of caffeine must be thoroughly reinvestigated in the light of this new knowledge.

"Among the more common symptoms are a lack of energy, undue readiness of fatigue, disinclination to activity, headache, pain in the back, disturbed sleep, insomnia, fullness after eating, dyspepsia, constipation, palpitation . . ." No, these were not intended to be symptoms of hyperinsulinism. When this list was compiled, not only hyperinsulinism but insulin itself had never been heard of. These symptoms are quoted from a widely used medical dictionary published in 1906 and are descriptive of *"neurasthenia,* a group of symptoms resulting from debility or exhaustion of the nerve-centers."

Those readers who are fifty or over undoubtedly will remember that in their youth it would be said, "Oh, I hope she doesn't marry *him,*" or, *"He'll* never hold *that* job." And the explanation given, almost always with a faint trace of contempt in the voice, was: "My dear, he's a hopeless *neurasthenic."* Today one does not hear so much about neurasthenia, which to many was just a polite, euphemistic way of calling someone "lazy and good for nothing."

With the advent of Sigmund Freud and his popularization by disciples and misinterpreters, the neurasthenic, like his brother the hapless neurotic, was pounced upon by the psychoanalysts, and his debilitated or exhausted nerves, which medicine had signally failed to cure, were ascribed to trauma deeply buried in his subconscious.

It now seems fairly obvious that the low blood sugar induced by hyperinsulinism would be more likely to affect the nerve tissue adversely than almost any other part of the body. As long ago as 1934 A. T. Cameron, describing the effects of insulin shock, wrote, "the symptoms are at least in part due to the fact that the central nervous system is particularly susceptible to glucose starvation having no store of carbohydrates." [7] Harris himself noted that among the "varied and fantastic" manifestations under which hyperinsulinism may masquerade are the "nervous syndromes [groups of symptoms] such as psychasthenia, neurasthenia, muscular asthenia, migraine, petit mal, narcolepsy, epilepsy, and psychosis." [8] In July, 1942, Rennie and Howard [9] reported on studies they had made of low blood sugar and tension depression in neuropsychiatric cases. And in December of the same year Dr. Sidney A. Portis, of Michael Reese Hospital and the College of Medicine of the University of Illinois, delivered an address to the opening meeting of the American Psychosomatic Society on "A Mechanism of Fatigue in Neuropsychiatric Patients," [10] in which he gave a preliminary report on the studies he and Dr. I. H. Zitman had made of low blood sugar in the type of patient whom we used to call neurasthenic. Continuing his work in this field, Dr. Portis reported twice in 1944 and twice in 1950.[11] What follows is a digest of this work of the last eight years.

Dr. Portis describes the large group of patients he first studied as exhibiting an "asthenic syndrome," the outstanding feature of this group of symptoms being "apathy, loss of zest, a general let-down feeling of aimlessness, a revulsion against the routine of everyday life, be it occupational activity or household duties." Another constant symptom reported is "fatigue, chronic or appearing in acute attacks." It has routine features. It is present as a rule on awakening, becomes slightly more severe by midmorning, temporarily improves after luncheon, and is most marked in midafternoon. Practically always there is complete relief after the heavy evening meal. The patient may awake with a severe headache, which is manifest also during the midafternoon fatigue. Along with this chronic fatigue there may be "acute attacks of extreme weakness, tremulousness, sweating, and vertigo. At times a feeling of 'lightheadedness' may be manifest. The acute attacks may be associated with anxiety of fainting or free floating anxiety." We recognize these symptoms as being typical of the milder form of functional hyperinsulinism.

Dr. Portis became interested in the subject because in a patient referred to him by a neuropsychiatrist the outstanding symptom was "so-called pernicious inertia." Dr. Portis is not a psychiatrist. Though he admits to "a great deal of sympathy with psychiatry and understands some of the dynamics," he is more "interested in mechanism and what goes on in the body." [12] And it is in connection with the mechanism of hyperinsulinism that he has made a unique and important contribution.

It is a popular belief that long-continued worry and anxiety may bring on such diseases as cancer and peptic ulcer. There is no direct scientific evidence of this. There is, however, considerable psychiatric and even medical literature on the effect of emotional impulses on the somatic system. "It is well known," says Dr. Portis, "that continued physiologic activity in a tissue may lead to either hypertrophy or hyperplasia, depending upon the type of tissue." Hypertrophy is an increase in the size of a tissue or organ that occurs independently of the growth of the body. Hyperplasia is an excessive development of a tissue due to an increase in the number of its cells.

As far back as 1927, J. La Barre and his associates had performed a series of experiments on dogs which revealed the role of the central nervous system in the control of pancreatic secretions. From these studies made in France we know that the pancreas, which is an end organ, is subject to stimulation through the *vagus*, the pneumogastric nerve which originates in the medulla oblongata and is distributed by many branches to the ear, pharynx, larynx, heart, lungs, esophagus, and stomach. Portis made the bold assumption that the low blood sugar of his psychoneurotic patients was due to a long-continued stimulation of the right vagus nerve. "The assumption was based upon the hypothesis that emotional processes occur somewhere in the highly integrated cortical and that the emotional impulses first go through the hypothalamus [a group of ganglia—the nervous system's switchboard—on the ventral side of the brain] and are relayed to the sympathetic and parasympathetic portions of the automatic nervous system. . . . this stimulation might lead to increased activity and irritability of the cells of the islands of Langerhans." This "might be temporary or prolonged, depending on the degree and duration of the . . . emotional impulses."

To test the validity of his assumptions, Dr. Portis studied a large group of patients "whose outstanding symptom was fatigue which could not be explained by thorough physical and routine laboratory investigation," including a determination of their fasting blood sugar levels. This varied in the one hundred and fifty-seven patients from normal through somewhat subnormal to definitely low values. Largely because their attacks of fatigue came on at regular intervals related to their mealtimes, he made further blood sugar level tests. His experience and conclusion that a single determination of blood sugar is meaningless are in complete agreement with ours.

At this point it should be pointed out that Dr. Portis did not employ the six-hour Glucose Tolerance Test with which you are now familiar. In that test the glucose is administered orally. Dr. Portis felt that oral administration might prejudice the results. "Gastrointestinal motility is readily influenced by emotional factors and the rate of absorption of dextrose [glucose] from the gastrointestinal tract is affected by motility and by cellular changes in the wall of the intestine." Instead he used a three-hour test in which the glucose (only 50 grams) was administered intravenously. (See Figure 9, p. 123.) He felt this had a further advantage over the oral test in that "the initial increase of blood sugar is far greater with the intravenous than with the oral test, so that one can logically expect a greater immediate response in secretion of insulin." We, on the other hand, prefer the oral test because it avoids the necessity of preparing a sterile solution and it spares the patient a puncture of his vein. Furthermore, the liver normally gets its glucose through the portal vein and in this test it reaches its destination through the hepatic artery. Since the insulin gets to the liver through the portal vein in the oral test, we feel that it more closely approximates physiological conditions. It is not too important, however, which test is used, provided the investigator confines himself to one procedure which will give him results from which he can draw comparisons. The three-hour intravenous test gives about the same results as the slower oral test, if we compare proportionate fractions of the test period.

Dr. Portis tested nine hundred and twenty-nine patients. Their blood sugar levels were determined in the fasting state and then one-half, one, two, and three hours after 50 grams of glucose solution were injected. "In not one of these nine hundred and twenty-nine patients did the third-hour level reach the original fasting level. In the one hundred and fifty-seven persons of the fatigue group, as distinct from the seven hundred and seventy-two having other than fatigue symptoms, the reading for the first thirty minutes was so low that the curves were 'flat' in comparison with the curves of both normal persons and persons without fatigue as predominating symptoms."

These fatigue patients differ from other hyperinsulinism patients both in their symptoms and in the greater "flatness" of the curves derived from their Glucose Tolerance Tests. Fatigue, and not hunger, is the predominating symptom. Though some of the fatigue patients also had weakness, tremulousness, sweating, vertigo, and lightheadedness as previously noted, only a very few had apprehension. One, a physician, had developed phobias. A twenty-year-old boy who had the lowest fasting blood sugar level, the "flattest" curve, and the lowest third-hour reading—all below 60 mg. per cent (anything below 70 mg. is subnormal)—exhibited extreme shyness, could not concentrate, and showed definite schizoid tendencies. (Statistics indicate that low blood sugar is characteristic of schizophrenia.)

Dr. Portis believes that this greater "flatness" of the fatigue curves is due to the stimulus of the right vagus nerve affecting the insulin secretion of the islands of Langerhans to such an extent that the usual initial rise in blood sugar is checked.

[114]

With this in mind, the following test was made with fifteen of the first fifty-five fatigue patients.

"A sample of the fasting blood was taken. The patient was then given ⅟₅₀ grain [1.3 mg.] of atropine sulfate hypodermically. After a half hour for adequate pharmacologic action of the drug, another blood sample was withdrawn. Immediately thereafter 50 per cent dextrose was injected as in the previous test, which had given 'flat' curves, and blood samples were withdrawn at the usual intervals. In these fifteen atropinized patients, the thirty-minute blood sugar level resembled that of normal persons. Because of the uniformity of results in this group, I felt that there was no need to subject a large group to this test."

Delving into the histories of his one hundred and fifty-seven fatigue patients, Dr. Portis found this to be the common denominator of their life situations: they were all people who lacked interest in their work because they had been forced into it by others or by such circumstances as extreme necessity, duty, pride, or insecurity. In each case there was also something else that each person would have liked to do better than what he was doing.

"Frustrated in their natural inclinations, these patients develop a protest reaction against their perfunctory activities."

When a life situation disturbs the patient and destroys his interest in his job, he goes on an "emotional sit-down strike" against the boredom of routine chores. The effort to do his job becomes too great because "zest, enthusiasm, interest" tone up the automatic nervous system, whose main function "is to adapt the internal vegetative functions of the organism to the tasks he is called upon to perform." Just as fear and rage tone up a man to fight, to defend himself, to escape, or otherwise to meet some special vital emergency, so it seems that "a keen enthusiastic striving for a goal may have a similar, more prolonged but less intensive tuning-up

[115]

effect on the internal vegetative processes. It is well known that perfunctory activity performed without emotional participation is more fatiguing than even strenuous activity performed with emotional participation. Clinical observations seem to indicate that fatigue and apathy developing during activity performed without interest are not merely subjective emotional states but are based on the lack of adaptation of the carbohydrate metabolism to the effort required from the organism."

In other words, to do work adequately, whether it be mental, manual, or a combination of the two, requires a blood sugar level high enough to supply the normal demands of muscle, nerve, and brain cells. Without that proper level of blood sugar, work is not performed economically. A strain is placed upon the functioning of the body and brain which becomes progressively injurious to them. The brain, especially, needs sugar at all times. What maintains the blood sugar at a proper level is apparently a proper balance between the sugar-repressive functions of insulin secreted in the islands of Langerhans of the pancreas and the sugar-releasing functions of the hormones from the adrenal cortex.

In normal, routine operations of work and of play it is the emotions of interest, zest, and enthusiasm that stimulate the secretion of the cortical hormones. In special emergencies it is fear and rage that stimulate the secretion of all of the body's "emergency" hormones. When the stimulus of zest is lacking and work is nevertheless performed, fatigue results and "the resulting fatigue gives further excuse for regressive wishes and thus a vicious circle is initiated." It is the vicious circle of hyperinsulinism, a condition of chronic partial sugar starvation which must become progressively worse unless that vicious circle is broken by placing the victim on the proper diet.

The proper diet is a matter about which Dr. Portis and the medical member of this team of authors do not see eye to eye

[116]

in every detail. There is absolute agreement, however, on fundamentals: no sugar, no quickly absorbable carbohydrates, a good breakfast, a snack between breakfast and luncheon, and another in midafternoon, and especially at bedtime. They differ somewhat as to how this dietary result is to be obtained. Dr. Portis utterly forbids alcohol and tobacco but is more lenient in regard to some of the common starchy foods. He also permits coffee. He overcomes the effects of the starches and caffeine by administering atropine or some other belladonna preparation, which depresses the activity of the islands of Langerhans through the involuntary nervous system. Dr. Abrahamson, on the other hand, feels that the rigid diet enables the patient to accomplish his aim—quieting the oversensitive insulin apparatus—without the use of drugs. We cannot and should not take medicine indefinitely, and it is better, he feels, not to use any drugs routinely, since they require another adjustment when they are abandoned. As far as smoking is concerned, he is in complete agreement with Dr. Portis in forbidding any smoking before meals. As a matter of fact, one cigarette before breakfast does more harm to anybody than twenty afterward. He feels that the harm done to frayed nerves by withholding the soothing pleasure of smoking can be greater than that produced by an occasional smoke.

Smoking, of course, is not *good* for anyone. In considering its harm one must make a distinction between the average "pack-a-day" smoker and the "chain" smoker—the moderate smoker and the individual who smokes almost throughout his waking hours, consuming two or more packages of cigarettes a day. American businessmen (about whom we shall have much to say) as a class are among the chain smokers. According to one authority,[13] 62 per cent of them smoke more than the average pack a day, 27 per cent smoke two, and 21 per cent more than two packages a day! Such excessive smoking permits a great deal more tars and acids, as well as nicotine, to be absorbed into the system and consequently is far more

[117]

harmful than the average person's moderate smoking. Raymond Pearl, one of the greatest investigators of longevity, has noted that one of every five heavy smokers between the ages of thirty and fifty dies before his time.[14]

While a minute quantity of concentrated nicotine is fatal (in solution, for example, nicotine is used as an insecticide), the amount in tobacco smoke is negligible. It is the tars and acids in the smoke that are harmful. We suggest that our readers try some of the denicotinized cigarettes that are on the market. You will find, we believe, that they produce even more tongue bite than ordinary, untreated cigarettes. In our opinion such removal of nicotine is of negligible value.

The caffeine in ordinary coffee and other caffeineated beverages, however, is completely absorbed by the body, and consequently all such drinks should be avoided.

The proof of any diet is in the eating. Both of these diets have proved to be eminently successful in the treatment of patients with low blood sugar induced by overactive islands of Langerhans. Both avoid or, in Dr. Portis', correct for foods which would induce a sudden rise in blood sugar and thus stimulate the islands of Langerhans, and both provide the correct food frequently enough to level off the drops that tend to follow meals.

A generation ago, Americans sat down to breakfasts which continental Europeans considered monstrous. The British have always been hearty eaters. Perhaps Americans on the farms, in villages, and in small towns still eat those old-time breakfasts. We don't know. We are city dwellers. But we do know that in urban areas and industrial areas among the multitude who "go to work"—and that is overwhelmingly the largest part of the population—a decent breakfast fit to cement body and mind together with sufficient blood sugar is rapidly becoming extinct. Many a young female careerist considers black coffee and cigarettes the proper way to break a twelve-hour fast and equip herself for the morning's work. The office worker doing this only slows the wheels of commerce in addition to injuring her health. The industrial worker also causes accidents. Dr. Portis has written about the relation between fatigue states and industrial accidents and has shown that a good breakfast and frequent feedings throughout the day are essential to the prevention of accidents.

"A canvas of 50,000 students from first grade through college revealed the startling fact that 65 per cent habitually ate a breakfast entirely inadequate for their physical needs and 16 per cent ate no breakfast at all." [15] The result is the inattention and poor scholarship of which present-day teachers complain. "Army efficiency engineers, investigating almost 1000 accident cases in ordnance depots, recently found that a large majority of the injured workers had come to their jobs without breakfast; resulting fatigue and carelessness had struck them down." [16]

According to Dr. E. V. McCollum of Johns Hopkins University, "hidden hunger" is a pernicious malady. *Hidden hunger* is indeed an apt description of the vague discomfort that afflicts the fatigue patient who, though unaware of it, is as in need of food as the ravenously hungry victim of a more pronounced hyperinsulinism.[17]

That hackneyed expression, "the tired businessman," is not merely a humorous quip, but the simple truth. The executive group comprising the managers of our large corporations are so fatigued that they are dying at a rate in excess of, and an age that is younger than, that of the general population. During the decade from 1940 to the present time, "industry has come to recognize that the toll of death and disability in the management group is excessive." In 1944 General Motors reported that one hundred and eighty-nine of the corporation's management group had died in the preceding five years.[18]

[119]

"The Life Extension Institute reported that of 1000 holders of life insurance policies in amounts of $25,000 or over who had received extensive examination since January 1, 1938 . . . 79 per cent were found to have physical impairments (18.5 per cent of which were high blood pressure and 22 per cent abnormalities of the heart)." In May, 1950, Dr. S. C. Franco reported finding major disease in 25 per cent of all executives receiving periodic health examinations.[19] Finally, *Fortune* in an article, "Why Executives Drop Dead," quoted the Life Extension Examiners of New York to the effect that "60 per cent of the executive group examined had conditions requiring a physician's attention, the larger part of them of a cardiovascular nature." [20] It has remained for Dr. Sidney A. Portis to call attention to conditions among younger executives that "if permitted to go unrecognized, may produce morbidity and mortality of a degree similar to that already reported." [21]

In a paper read before the Section on Preventive and Industrial Medicine and Public Health at the Ninety-ninth Annual Session of the American Medical Association in San Francisco on June 29, 1950,[22] Dr. Portis stated that exhaustion in relatively young executives "has not been stressed by other investigators in surveys previously published." For many years Dr. Portis has been seeing "executives in their early forties and fifties who became utterly exhausted." He made a study of fifty such executive patients all under the age of fifty, and he discovered that "in 60 per cent of the group fatigue was one of the outstanding complaints." He subjected these business executives to the three-hour Dextrose Tolerance Test. "In 58 per cent of the entire group of executive patients, the third-hour blood sugar level was below the initial level determined during fasting. In some instances there was a drop of 30 to 40 mg. per 100 cc., while in others the drop was between 5 and 15 mg. One severely fatigued executive showed a fasting level of 87 mg. per 100 cc." which is not below normal, but "at the third hour his blood sugar level had dropped to 44 mg."

In previous studies Dr. Portis has shown that this relatively low blood sugar is due to an overstimulation of the islands of Langerhans—hyperinsulinism—"mediated by the parasympathetic nervous system via the vagi. Blocking of the vagus nerves with atropine sulfate throughout the twenty-four-hour period has resulted in the elimination of this drop in blood sugar values. Several patients who have had a vagectomy for treatment of peptic ulcer have also shown a diminution of their drop in blood sugar values.

Dr. Portis' studies have shown that when the amount of sugar circulating in the blood is inadequate, "the brain does not function properly, the patient becomes high-strung and easily fatigued, and the body does not maintain its competence." An almost constant feature in the life situations of the tired young businessmen whom Dr. Portis treated "was a loss of zest, loss of enthusiasm," and the replacement of such beneficial emotions with "boredom and antipathy for their jobs, business superiors, and associates."

He tells us that psychological studies have revealed that "as a rule" the executives who develop these physical symptoms of fatigue are "dependent men whose insecurities and feelings of inferiority are great." This intense fear of being found inadequate, rather than real joy in their work, is the driving force of insatiable ambition. The machine of the body is being driven by a lean mixture, by the wrong kind of mixture. The result is injury that reveals itself eventually "in symptoms in the gastrointestinal, cardiovascular, respiratory, and neuro-muscular systems."

On the surface these executives appear to get along with each other. But "their relations to their families are frequently hostile, so that their wives and children are injured. Frenzy

[121]

and repressed aggression . . . are present in most such persons. . . . Their capacity for getting pleasure out of life is limited." The executive lives with apprehension or fear that pride in the accomplishments of yesterday will be wiped out by tomorrow's failure.

This is all well illustrated in a case history which Dr. Portis gives in his report [23] and which we here quote in full:

REPORT OF CASE

A business executive, 37 years of age, had felt well until nine days prior to consultation, when at 3:30 P.M., as he was walking through the factory, he suddenly felt light-headed, began to perspire and noticed quickening of his heartbeat. His legs felt weak and he had to sit down. The company physician found his systolic blood pressure at that time to be 110. He was taken to the hospital, where an electrocardiogram and blood count were within normal limits. He remained in the hospital only one hour. However, after that time he continued to feel weak and tired; he became light-headed when up and around but felt normal when lying down. It tired him to walk one block, but he experienced no shortness of breath. He stated that on the day preceding the onset of these symptoms he thought he had overexerted himself. His muscles ached and felt dull, as though they were tired, and he noticed a peculiar sensation over the middle anterior part of the chest. This sensation disappeared almost entirely, yet walking a half block still brought on a "choked-up" feeling.

Physical examination revealed nothing of clinical significance. Except for the intravenous dextrose tolerance test below, thorough laboratory and roentgenologic studies gave normal results. The dextrose tolerance curve, however, resembled the so-called "flat curve" which we had previously observed in fatigue patients. This flat curve is characterized by a lower than normal level at the half-hour determination and failure of the blood sugar to return to the fasting level in three hours.

[122]

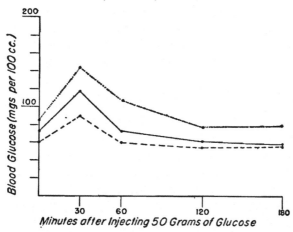

9—*Intravenous Glucose Tolerance Test in Fatigue*

The broken line is the curve obtained in the case cited.
The dotted line is an average of normal controls.
The solid line gives the mean values for Portis' "fatigue cases."

Because we were interested in discovering what precipitated the acute condition which had persisted for nine days, we inquired into the psychological factors which might have brought about the breakdown. We found that the patient was employed by a concern which had decided shortly after the war that a plant in a small town would be better suited than their current plant to their specifications and purposes. They moved their key employees into a small community, built homes for them and set them to work. For the first few years of operation of this plant, operations went at top speed and with the smoothness of a fine watch. However, after four or five years the management found that efficiency in the plant was lowered. There had been no change in the capabilities of the executives; they were still young and still able to do a job, but they now were becoming tired, befuddled and irritable. The chief executive, at the age of 37, had noticed that in the early midportion of the afternoon he experienced acute fatigue. He began to suffer from precordial distress; he resorted to chain smoking and felt ex-

[123]

hausted when he came home at the end of the day. His wife was struggling along with three children and no diversification in her day's work. When she would have liked a break in the monotony of her domestic life, she found that her young husband was content to sit around and recover from the fatigue of his daily efforts in the plant. This furnished a desirable escape mechanism for him. The situation was aggravated by lack of adequate social outlets, since the couple could not become too closely associated with the younger executives because of the danger that such personal relations would be detrimental to efficiency in business.

Analysis of this executive's life situations showed him to have the aggressive, dependent type of personality commonly seen among executives. The patient's mother had died when he was 9 years of age, and he had been passed from one relative to another until his father remarried two years later. He had been a football player and had subsequently married, had three children and become successful, rising to be executive director of a plant employing 400 workers. The onset of his complaint coincided with the development of a fatigue syndrome in his wife, who was distinctly bored and unhappy with life in a small town and who complained bitterly of the lack of social and intellectual diversion.

What does all this add up to? On the one hand, the business of the plant was conducted more efficiently and production costs were lower than in its previous location. On the other hand, at the end of five years its top executives were distinctly bored and tired and sooner or later became inefficient. Of course management and business must get a fair return on their capital investments or they will not be able to enlarge, modernize or expand their plants. But business should realize that highly developed, highly skilled workers must have some chance for diversion in their life outside the plant. This may mean that management may not profitably locate plants in areas where the labor market is good if the price they have to pay is a breakdown in the efficiency of their top executives.

[124]

Fifty-five executives under the age of fifty were referred to Dr. Portis by various corporations for "prophylactic examination." These were not men who considered themselves ill, nor were they sent to him because someone else thought so. They were sent for a check-up. They were given a complete physical examination including such laboratory tests as: "urine and stool analyses, complete serologic study, blood counts with differential, electrocardiogram, 2-meter roentgenogram of the chest to determine the exact size of the heart and condition of the lungs and determination of the basal metabolic rate." In addition, each man was interviewed concerning his previous clinical history and also what may be called his social history: his childhood, education, family, environment, jobs previously held and reasons for leaving, marital status, home life, friends, vacations, relations to his superiors, equals, and those under him—in short, everything that could be found out about him.

Dr. Portis reports that the average businessman does not go to the doctor of his own accord. Of these fifty-five who had been sent to him, twenty-eight or 50.5 per cent had not had a physical examination in two years. Another 27.3 per cent had not had one in five years. Yet "only 5.4 per cent of these men were considered entirely normal without any physical defect." Some 29.1 per cent had hypertension; 27.4 per cent had obesity. The electrocardiograph showed abnormalities in 12.7 per cent, and another 10.9 per cent on the borderline of abnormality. Of these men who thought themselves well, 10.9 per cent had fatigue, as compared with 60 per cent of those who had gone to the doctor of their own accord because they knew they were sick. The survey "revealed two important facts: first the lack of adequate medical study prior to this study, and second, the high incidence of asymptomatic organic disease"—diseases of the cardiovascular system which are without symptoms. Dr. Portis concludes that the average man or woman "thinks his or her organs are superior, although he knows less about the workings of the human body than he does about an automobile. He does not take into consideration the fact that, although one can get new parts for an automobile, no new parts have been developed for the human machine at the present writing. The intelligent person who has an automobile will take that machine into a service station every one or two thousand miles to have it oiled, greased, and checked, but he does not give equivalent care to his own body."

By now we have reached a phase in the development of the concept which enables us to clarify some of the uncertainties with which we were confronted. To return to the classification of the disorders of the islands of Langerhans, we have, in the descending order of severity:

1. Malignant insulomas
2. Benign insulomas
3. Functional hyperinsulinism

Now, the latter group can be subdivided into:

a. Manifest hyperinsulinism
b. Subclinical hyperinsulinism

In manifest hyperinsulinism the classical (if such a term can be applied to a condition of so recent discovery) symptoms of hyperinsulinism, such as rabid hunger, faintness, etc., come to the fore. In subclinical hyperinsulinism the degree of lowering of the blood sugar is so slight that the usual symptoms of the disturbance are wanting. While the normal blood sugar is around 140 mg. per 100 cc., in the subclinical hyperinsulinism state it hovers around 80 or even lower. Thus, the victim of this abnormality suffers from a chronic partial glucose starvation. He feels more or less as normal people do if they go without food for several hours. His human machine is being run on a lean mixture. Since sugar is the chief fuel for

[126]

all the activities of the body, the effect will be felt throughout the body. Local conditions will determine exactly which part or function of the body will be most affected, which is why hyperinsulinism can produce such variegated symptoms. And this is also why it has failed to be recognized so often. We submit that it is a most widespread condition because of the excessive consumption of caffeine in the United States. One thing is certain—it is far more common than its opposite, diabetes.

6

Alcohol
and Alcoholics

ALCOHOL, STIMULANT OR DEPRESSANT?
—COMPULSIVE DRINKING—THE "PROB-
LEM DRINKER"—ALCOHOLICS ANONY-
MOUS—ALCOHOLISM, DIABETES, AND HY-
PERINSULINISM—MORE CASE HISTORIES

THERE HAVE BEEN drinks, drinkers, and drunks
on earth since long before the dawn of history. The custom of
drinking alcoholic beverages must be at least thirty thousand
years old. Wine- and beer-making are probably man's oldest
arts. In spite of this antiquity, we still do not know why a
majority can drink without getting habitually drunk and a
minority cannot. Though there are many theories, there is no
one, officially accepted, scientific hypothesis to explain alcoholism.

This is largely because scientific knowledge of alcohol has
come to us belatedly. Primitive men thought that these ex-
hilarating beverages were a gift from the gods, and they called
whatever it was in them that made them that way, "spirits."
At first they drank these beverages communally and ceremoni-
ally. With appropriate rituals, incantations by priests and
medicine men, dancing by maidens and youths, and recita-

tions by the bards, they got together and drank until they were all drunk. Individual drinking was taboo.

This ritualistic and orgiastic drinking survived into Greco-Roman times in the cults of Dionysus and Bacchus. Something of it survives even today in the reunions of college classes and the get-togethers of fraternal orders. But in the Greece of Pericles and the Rome of Caesar wine-drinking with meals had already become an item of gracious living. This custom of using fine wines as a condiment has spread from the Latin countries throughout the civilized world. In Rome nearly everyone got drunk on certain special occasions, but the habitual drunkard was frowned upon. They gave him a preview of our present-day emetine treatment. Emetine is the drug which makes one violently sick, so that the patient vomits the drink that is given him and comes to associate drinking with getting sick. The Roman version was to make the drunkard dip his cup into a huge bowl of wine with eels swimming about in it.

The excesses of the lusty, ale-drinking Teutonic barbarians who began to infiltrate the decaying Roman Empire actually shocked Pliny, who was one of the first to write about drinking as a social problem. But getting drunk and staying drunk most of the time was considered a breach of manners and good taste rather than a breach of morals until after the Protestant Reformation and the advent of the Puritans who looked upon everything pleasurable as sinful.

By this time, when the movement toward Prohibition really began in the Western world, we had learned to distill from the Arabs. With this knowledge had come that of the nature of *alcohol,* which is an Arabic word. It is interesting to note that the Arabs not only taught us how to make the more potent distilled liquors but introduced the Abyssinian beverage caffa to the world. The Mohammedans began drinking coffee to keep awake during their lengthy religious services. From them it spread to Venice and eventually to all Europe, and so to

America where most of it now is grown in Brazil and consumed in the United States.

The alcohol problem never had a chance once the Puritans got hold of it. It was inevitable that science would be excluded from its consideration until the moral utopians had had their day. To paraphrase Winston Churchill, never before had a well-meaning few done so much harm to so many as in the noble experiment of Prohibition. It set us back at least a generation. Quite apart from its enormous by-products of social evil, it perpetuated the point of view expressed by William Graham Sumner when he said, "If a drunkard is in the gutter, that is where he belongs," and added to it, "until a policeman comes along and carries him off to jail."

It wasn't until after Repeal and the discrediting of the moralist point of view that science was at last able and encouraged to take a hand. Perhaps science which had given us the miracles of our modern age would succeed with alcoholics where everything else had failed.

The notion that alcoholism is a disease and not a form of moral depravity has long been held among an enlightened minority. Even in ancient times there were some who regarded alcoholic intoxication as a form of temporary insanity. In Sanskrit, for example, the word for alcoholic intoxication and for insanity is the same. But widespread acceptance of the idea, that alcoholism is a disease like any other noncommunicable disease, has come in this country only since Repeal and especially in the last fifteen years. In that time, however, mostly in the decade 1940–50, a revolution has taken place in public thinking concerning alcoholism. Science has come up with nearly all the answers except one. As C. Lester Walker has aptly expressed it,[1] "We are still trying to find out what puts the drunkard in the gutter in the first place, but we no longer feel that, once there, it is the inevitable or proper place for him." And once rid of the idea that the only way to prevent *some* people from getting drunk was to prohibit *all* people from drinking, only then did we begin to make real progress toward solution of the problem.

Just how much of a problem is it? Of the current estimate of sixty-five million drinkers of alcoholic beverages in the United States, some four million are alcoholics, according to Yale University's famed Section on Alcoholic Studies of the Laboratory of Applied Physiology. "This means that there are probably 20,000,000 people, nonalcoholics among whom these alcoholics live and have their being, who are more or less seriously affected by the alcoholics' behavior." [2]

The direct and indirect cost to the nation of alcoholism has been estimated by various authorities at between three quarters of a billion and a billion dollars a year. This is a sum large enough to make it worth while to spend at least a quarter of a billion on research for a few years to prevent it. Especially is this advisable in view of the fact that the number of alcoholics in proportion to the total number who drink is increasing all the time. The grand total of the nation's imbibing of alcoholic beverages—in spite of the ravages of Prohibition which taught women to drink as they never had before—is below its peak of two and a half gallons of absolute alcohol a year for every adult. The crest of our drinking was reached between the turn of the century and the beginning of World War I. By 1940 it had declined 40 per cent, but now in 1950 it is 30 per cent higher than a decade ago.

One of the jobs well done by science in the last decade has been to relieve the public mind of its many glaring misconceptions concerning alcohol. Many of these downright lies were fostered by the Prohibitionists—good people who saw nothing wrong in using foul means to attain what they believed was a worthy end. Let us take a brief refresher course in the fundamentals of our scientific knowledge of the subject. To begin with, "The subtle alchemist that in a trice Life's leaden metal into gold transmute," is ethyl alcohol, chemically C_2H_5OH—nothing but oxygen, hydrogen, and carbon. The same elements are found in sugar, starch, and fats. In fact, chemically speaking, alcohol and water are related. "Alcohol, whatever the kind, has an oxygen-hydrogen combination called the -OH group, exactly as does water, HOH. Hence alcohol tends to dissolve in water. One might think of water as an alcohol, hydroalcohol 100 per cent pure. The kind of alcohol one has depends on the kind of tail one puts on the -OH dog. Attach . . . CH_3 and the result is methyl or wood alcohol which blinds and kills. Attach C_2H_5 and it is ethyl or grain alcohol, the age-old consoler of mankind." [3, 4]

This substance, ethyl alcohol, is produced in nature by the process called alcoholic fermentation, in which the sugar in fruits is changed into alcohol and carbon dioxide by the action of yeast, a simple form of plant life which will grow in sugar under the right conditions. The spores of this plant are airborne. Ethyl alcohol is not a poison like its cousin methyl alcohol. It is a *food*. Each ounce, by weight, of absolute alcohol has 210 calories. This is exactly the same as a half pound of sea bass. A better source of comparison with other foods is this: 1 gram of alcohol yields 7.0 calories, whereas 1 gram of carbohydrate or protein gives only 4.1 calories. Alcohol is exceeded only by fats which furnish 9.3 calories per gram. Like other foods, alcohol burns in the body.

It is for this reason that a drunk can go for days and even weeks on nothing but alcohol without starving to death. No one can flourish on alcohol, however, because it contains nothing but calories—no vitamins whatever. A lengthy diet of alcoholic beverages will produce only the diseases of vitamin deficiency such as beriberi and pellagra.

Drinking in moderation never harmed anyone, and even drinking habitually to excess does not *cause* any of the ills it was once supposed to, such as insanity by "corroding the cells of the brain"—a favorite with the Munchhausens of Prohibition. It does not *cause* kidney trouble, hardening of the arteries, high blood pressure, cancer, or stomach ulcers. It may be associated, however, with ulcer, but for a reason to be discussed later. It does not *cause* cirrhosis of the liver. (Mohammedans, who do not drink at all, have more cirrhosis than we do.) But there is some association between cirrhosis and alcoholism, probably of a nutritional nature.

Drinking does not injure the germ plasm, so that alcoholism cannot be hereditary. What *is* inherited is *something* which predisposes one toward alcoholism. Raymond Pearl found that potential alcoholics seem to run in certain families whose other individual members are usually total abstainers, whereas the "average" family of moderate drinkers seldom if ever tends to produce a drunkard. Pearl also showed that both alcoholics and abstainers are shorter lived than average moderate drinkers.

One of our most cherished illusions is that alcohol is a stimulant. IT IS NOT. It does not "pep you up," make you stronger, more clever, or more efficient. It is a narcotic, a "descending central nervous system *depressant*." It attacks the highest brain centers first, then works downward through the central nervous system, putting to sleep and paralyzing the areas of the brain that control muscular coordination, speech, sight, and other sensory centers, and finally, the vital centers in the medulla become so impaired that the alcoholic sinks into a stupor, which may end in death by *respiratory paralysis*. Alcohol is also the only sedative that will effectively cure the hang-over jitters of overindulgence in it. As a painkiller it is three times more effective than aspirin. Unfortunately, if you take enough alcohol to dull a really bad pain, you are drunk.

What alcohol actually does is to create the illusion of stimulation by deadening the critical faculties. Alcohol makes you think you are better than you are. It breaks the chains of your inhibitions, freeing your behavior from any consideration of anxiety as to what others will think of you. Dulling the mind's pains as well as the body's, erasing anxiety, apprehension,

[133]

and worry, alcohol suffuses the whole being with the glow of a wonderful expansiveness. The psychologists call it euphoria. *While the euphoria lasts,* you are the man of your dreams, only even more so.

In several university laboratories psychologists have conducted scientifically controlled tests which definitely prove that people do not function better, even after only a few drinks, than when perfectly sober. These tests have shown that the subjects' visual reactions are impaired by one third. Their ability to memorize poetry is cut in half. Their facility for solving mathematical problems is reduced 13 per cent, while their reasoning is subject to 67 per cent more errors. Even their muscular strength is decreased by 10 per cent, although the subjects are quite sure they feel less fatigued!

There are, however, a very few people whose reactions do improve after a *few* drinks. These are the very shy and inhibited persons whose inferiority sense makes them ill at ease and never at their potential best in the presence of others. The relaxing and disinhibiting effects of a *few* drinks bring these psychologically subnormal people up to par.

In spite of these exceptions and what still may be the reader's personal conviction—based upon the exhilaration felt following a few drinks after a trying day—alcohol actually anesthetizes the drinker as surely as ether. But alcohol puts one to sleep slyly and insidiously, as if it were doing the very opposite.

What is the composition of alcoholic beverages? The malt liquors—lager beer, ale, porter, and stout—have the lowest alcoholic content, about 4 to 4.5 per cent and never over 6 per cent. They also have considerable amounts of carbohydrate and very small amounts of protein, but no fat. The dry table wines—(red) Burgundy, claret, etc., and (white) sauterne, Rhine, etc.—have less carbohydrate and protein and more alcohol, about 10 per cent to 12 per cent. The fortified wines—sherry, port, madeira—if they are sweet, are highest in carbohydrate of any alcoholic beverage except the sweet cordials. The alcoholic content of the fortified wines is between 15 per cent and 20 per cent. The hard liquors—rum, gin, brandy, rye, bourbon, Irish, and Scotch—have no carbohydrate or protein whatever. Their alcoholic content varies from 35 per cent in Scotch, rum, and gin to 40 per cent in Irish, rye, and bourbon, and 45 per cent in vodka.

Now when we drink any of these alcoholic beverages, the carbohydrates (if any) and the negligible amounts of protein (if any) are digested just as in any other foods. While the carbohydrate is transformed into glucose, however, the alcohol does a very strange thing. It is *osmosed* through the walls of the stomach. About 22 per cent seeps right into the blood stream. When it gets to the heart it does another strange thing. Alcohol is no more a heart stimulant than it is a brain stimulant. It does not speed up the heart—it simply releases the controls and permits the heart to act practically as it pleases. It expands the blood vessels, so that more blood gets through. It is this increased circulation of the blood around the nerve centers of the brain that does the "intoxicating." At first it dulls that part of the brain which censors and inhibits our behavior. This sudden relaxation, after the worries, anxieties, and apprehensions to which flesh is heir, gives us that wonderful sense of release. An alcoholic once remarked that his idea of heaven would be to dwell eternally in the golden glow of well-being and self-esteem that follows the first drink and is so soon the memory that one tries in vain to recapture.

The drinks that follow the first one or two or three steadily increase the concentration of alcohol in the blood. The anesthetizing effect moves from one region of the brain to another. After the highest centers have been dulled and our judgment destroyed, gradually but inexorably the areas of muscular coordination, speech, and vision are affected. We begin to weave a little as we walk. We miss the end of our cigarette as we try to light it. Our speech becomes thick and slurred;

our vision is blurred and eventually doubled. Sooner or later, as the higher faculties that make us human are all put to sleep, we become animals. And finally, when the alcohol concentration in the blood reaches about ten ounces, we "pass out."

As we all know from observation, the pattern of intoxication varies enormously from person to person. These variations have been corroborated by studies. Seven per cent of a thousand drinkers were still sober with a .4 per cent concentration of alcohol in the blood. Ten and a half per cent were intoxicated with a concentration of only .05 per cent, or eight times less. In addition, there are factors apart from individual idiosyncrasy. One can drink a great deal more without becoming intoxicated, for example, if there is food in the stomach to absorb some of the alcohol.

Alcohol also increases the peripheral, or outside, circulation by which the nerves are fed. This would be beneficial but for the fact that as our drinks "wear off," the nerves are sealed up even tighter than they were before. This is what makes a hang-over such a horrible experience. Besides depleting the body's Vitamin B content, essential to the nerves, the alcohol also seals up the lifelines of the fuel supply, the peripheral circulation. And only alcohol itself will re-open them. This is why, until very recently, there was nothing but alcohol to assuage a hang-over. Today there is another remedy (which we shall discuss later), but it cannot be carried about as conveniently as an aspirin, or administered as easily as a few ounces of whisky.

A normal man may get drunk and suffer a hang-over. He tapers it off with "a hair of the dog that bit him"—a little liquor. By the next day he is a well man, his spree but a memory. He may not get drunk again for weeks, months, a year, or ever. The alcoholic, however, usually cannot get by the hangover of the "morning after." In curing it, he does more than simply taper off—he involves himself in a new drunken epi-

[136]

sode, and so on, day after day, until his funds are depleted or he lands in a hospital with delirium tremens. The hospital gets the alcohol out of his system and he leaves, still a little shaky, but sober. For a week or a month he doesn't touch the stuff. Then something happens. He meets a friend he hasn't seen for years and the happy reunion calls for a celebration. Or it is New Year's Eve, or he is invited to a very special cocktail party, or he is passing a bar, and for no apparent reason, he goes in to have "one—just one." Invariably the cycle of intoxication and hang-over is reinitiated.

What enslaves the alcoholic to a liquid which others can manage with pleasure and sometimes even profit? What compulsion relentlessly drives him to his own destruction? His family and friends implore him to stop drinking—in vain. Repeatedly he himself pauses to scream his abject shame and remorse. Surely there is no other disease like alcoholism. What causes it? How can it be cured?

While there is no officially accepted hypothesis to account for alcoholism, several have been submitted. They fall into three main categories: the psychological, the physiological, and a combination of the two. Once it was admitted that alcoholism was a disease and not a perverse moral depravity, the psychiatrists, the psychologists, and the psychoanalysts moved in and took over. This malady, so unlike any other, more akin to neurotic and psychotic states, surely was a mental and not a physical disease, and, as such, their province.

Under the lingering influence of the Freudians, the "flight-from-reality" hypothesis was most frequently ascribed to the alcoholic. He was running away from life, seeking nepenthe in alcohol. Why? Because—but now the psychological school spread out like an umbrella tree. He was running away from life because he was a rejected child. Unwanted and unloved, he recoiled from life. He was running away from life because he was a spoiled only child on whom his parents, especially his mother, had lavished so much love and devotion that the

[137]

grown man was emotionally still a child. Life frightened him, so he ran away from it. He sought to escape from life because it had become unbearable. He had a neurosis, a personality disturbance resulting from the fact that his beloved had jilted him, or married him and shattered his illusions about her. Or he had wanted to be a poet or an artist and had been forced by his father to go into the insurance business. He had wanted to be a composer; he had been forced to become a salesman. So he drank to hear the music he no longer heard at any other time. *Etcetera, etcetera, ad infinitum.*

It was a great hypothesis. It filled the coffers of the psychoanalysts probing for that hidden motive. The one about the spoiled only son almost made off with the band wagon. Statistics had buttressed it with respectability. Only sons were (and are) more likely to become drunkards than other men. There was, however, one fly in the psychological ointment. Even with the alcoholic's hidden motive removed, the victim of it still could not drink normally. After one drink he slipped right back into his ancient ways. That wise and mellow psychiatrist, the late Dr. Myerson, pronounced the hypothesis "inadequate."

A Roman Catholic priest, who has had vast experience with alcoholics, advanced an engaging hypothesis. "The alcoholic is not running away from life, he is seeking it, seeking it more abundantly. The typical alcoholic is not an inferior, but a superior person. He has a great driving force, a desire and a yearning for a more abundant life. The typical alcoholic is an extremist, a perfectionist. He works harder and plays harder than his normal friends. Physically, your alcoholic must be more full of life than the average or he couldn't take the beating he gives himself. Mentally, he is also usually better equipped than his non-alcoholic fellows. No matter what his occupation, you will find him near the top. He is nearly always someone who starts out with brilliant promise of greatness. How often you hear it said of him, 'if only he would quit drinking, he'd be at the top.'

"Early in his quest for the more abundant life, the alcoholic discovers alcohol. On his first sizable drink of this elixir, he experiences a high surge of feeling, a strong exaltation. 'This is it.' This is the life for which you have been seeking. This is Truth and Good. This is a glimpse of eternity. It almost says to him, 'This is a little bit of God.'

"And because there is an almost immediate let-down, because he feels his elation oozing away and he wants desperately to recapture it, he calls for another drink. This, however, may give him the lilt of the first drink, but in addition it gives him a further let-down, so trying vainly to re-glimpse eternity, he orders a third and a fourth and a fifth until he is unable to feel anything at all—at least for some time.

"The alcoholic does not often see clearly that he is looking for life. Too often he is told that he is running away from life —from what people are pleased to call *reality*. Eminent psychiatrists even tell it to him. But the inner voice continues to say that it isn't so. Consequently, he becomes utterly confused and bewildered or cynically skeptical of the opinions of all non-alcoholics or again even surly and resentful of them.

"In the process he may act the greatest Hamlet of his generation [John Barrymore], write many of the best works of fiction [Thomas Wolfe] or publish them [Horace Liveright], but little by little, slowly and inexorably, his life becomes unmanageable. His intellect and his will are no longer the captains of his soul. It is ethyl alcohol who rules. At last there may come the realization that he cannot find his happiness in alcohol. In his remorse he screams, 'this is *not* it. This is *not* Truth, *not* Good, *not* the more abundant life for which I am looking.' But he is powerless to do anything about it. The throne of his intellect and will has been usurped by a cruel tyrant who

[139]

holds him in the bondage of a vicious circle of physical allergy and mental obsession, of hang-over, bender, and hang-over, from which he cannot escape except in madness or death." [5]

Outstanding in the field of psychologists who have devoted themselves to the study and treatment of alcoholism is Dr. (PH.D.) Charles H. Durfee. Perhaps more than anyone else, he has taken a purely objective, scientific attitude toward the subject, unprejudiced by any conceptions from the past. He has collected an enormous amount of data, almost entirely the result of his own experience with alcoholics, and has developed an eminently successful method of treatment based on this material. Dr. Durfee believes that "drinkers are made, not born." While recognizing the existence of inherited and environmental predispositions, he believes that "excessive drinking is essentially a learned, inadequate way of reacting to personality difficulties—that drinking habits are acquired. Their correction, therefore, can be brought about only through a process of unlearning and re-education." [6]

Dr. Durfee is quite certain that there is not merely one "alcoholic type." The neurotic, who is fearful of life and running away from it, is one of many different kinds of people with different personality difficulties who may resort to alcohol. "No one is born an alcoholic and there is no such thing as an alcoholic type. There are only individuals who drink for various reasons." [7] In another place he wrote, "many excessive drinkers are otherwise well-adjusted people. . . . Such drinkers have learned to drink through drinking."

Inasmuch as alcohol is not a habit-forming drug (in the same sense as, for example, morphine or cocaine), it may seem strange that the alcoholic apparently has such an irresistible craving for it. This craving is physiological only as long as alcohol remains in his system. Once the last of it has been removed by oxidation, no physiological craving remains. According to Dr. Durfee, "The force of psychological

[140]

habituation, however, cannot be lightly discounted." [8] Else-where he wrote, "Psychological habituation is a significant factor in the drinking history of both the maladjusted personality and the normal person. More than any other causative element, routine drinking can make alcohol, a drug not physiologically addictive, the object of irresistible craving. We all know how disturbing even minor dislocations of routine can be—failing to get one's coffee or morning paper at breakfast, or missing a train. Alcohol, more intimately related to subjective and physical states such as worry, depression, and fatigue, is particularly suited to become a habit, especially if indulged in as a regular practice over a period of years. To psychological habituation must be added an acquired tolerance, so that increased quantities are necessary to produce the desired effect." [9] The desired effect, of course, is that feeling of lift and glow and release from worry, depression, and fatigue for which the alcoholic drink is taken.

Whether or not one can agree with Dr. Durfee's dictum that "the foundations of alcoholism are predominantly psychological," one cannot but be enormously grateful for the wealth of fact he has gathered and used to illuminate the physiological and psychological factors.

Among his many contributions to our knowledge of alcoholism is the remarkable list of signs and symptoms of what constitutes a "problem drinker," a phrase coined by Dr. Durfee and which he uses in preference to alcoholic. Some critics of Dr. Durfee aver that "problem drinker" is a Victorianesque euphemism for an economic elite which cannot stomach the harsh truth of "alcoholic." This is not the case. Dr. Durfee explains that " 'chronic alcoholic,' in law, in criminology, and in sociology, has assumed a strong suggestion of moral stigma." There is no doubt of it. With Alcoholics Anonymous, we believe that no stigma should be attached to the term. Every effort should be made to point out the patent absurdity and ignorance of such a stigma in dealing with a disease. For just as the diabetic cannot live without insulin, so the alcoholic cannot live with alcohol.

Dr. Durfee's reasons for coining the term, problem drinker, rather than bucking the current, were motivated by therapeutic experience. He found in treatment of "alcoholics" that this suggestion of "weakness and moral unfitness may do serious psychological harm to patient and therapist alike in discussing the problems posed by alcohol." Dr. Durfee defines the problem drinker as "a person in whose life drink overshadows, threatens, or has already destroyed what we consider normal living."

The first of Dr. Durfee's eight signs and symptoms is "to draw a blank"—that not uncommon experience in which, after a certain number of drinks, the drinker is intoxicated but maintains consciousness, apparently aware of what he is saying and doing, only to remember nothing whatever of what he has said or done the next day. This occurrence is a definite sign of physiological changes taking place within the drinker.

Dr. Durfee calls the second sign "extra-curricular drinks." This takes many forms, such as "pantry drinking" at parties; feeling the need for "a quick one" before the party or the meeting; or feeling that the drinks are too weak or served with too great an interval between them. These are all indications of the "incipient problem drinker."

The third sign is "an unwillingness to talk about liquor as a problem in his life," and "a readiness to accuse friends and family of imagined slights and wrongs."

The fourth is "rationalization." In the beginning this takes the form of finding all sorts of excuses for taking a drink. "When rationalization is carried over from justifying a few drinks to justifying a succession of drinks, with no considerable period of abstinence, then the familiar mental pattern of the problem drinker has taken shape."

"Unwillingness to attend meetings, dinners, and social functions where liquor is not served," the fifth sign, indicates "that alcohol has lost its true relative value to its victim." At this stage "the prospect of a drink is more pleasing than any other aspect of a party, a conference, a day or an hour of relaxation."

The sixth item, "change in the character of hang-overs," is momentous. On the "morning after," an ordinary heavy drinker has "a headache and marked fatigue. A chronic drinker's hang-overs, however, are like no other ailment known to man." In addition to such physical symptoms as extreme fatigue, with acute muscular pains, excruciating headache, butterflies in the chest, nausea, and belching, he is the prey of such psychological symptoms as "morbid apprehension, vague but inescapable fears, feelings of guilt and shame. He is about as thoroughly miserable as a human being can be." The things that used to mitigate his earlier hang-overs—"aspirin, black coffee, and fruit juices—" are of no use now. "Alcohol alone will temporarily bring relief. As the day progresses he will have to maintain a steady intake in order to feel normal. By nightfall he has a heavy concentration of alcohol in his bloodstream and is apt to end up in a rotation of maudlin, bitter, and unenjoyed drunkenness. After long years of drinking [other authorities specify an average of fifteen years for a man and ten for a woman], one of his sprees may culminate in delirium tremens or acute alcoholic hallucinosis."

Gastrointestinal disorders are the seventh group of signs and symptoms. "This is indicated by a failing appetite, particularly at the beginning of the day." As for the morning tremors and other hang-over symptoms, the alcoholic's cure for this is the eye opener, so that "he eats less and less, until alcohol becomes both food and drink to him. The result is a vitamin deficiency found in most excessive drinkers."

The eighth and final item on Dr. Durfee's list consists of two conditions—insomnia and irritability—"characteristic of the problem drinker," which "may have serious consequences psychologically both for himself and for his family." He concludes his listing of signs and symptoms with these words: "A person who finds himself with any one of these symptoms is in the gravest danger of becoming a true compulsive drinker. Could his state be made perfectly and fully clear to him at the onset of any of these results of drinking, he might be saved from the messy life that awaits him if he continues to drink. . . . A problem drinker can never drink again, even in moderation, without getting into difficulties. But he can learn to live and to enjoy life without alcohol." [10]

Dr. Durfee has put his rich experience to good use in operating Rocky Meadows Farm in the South County section of Rhode Island. For more than ten years this unique community has given the unhappy problem drinker a place, free from the restrictions of institutionalism, in which to unlearn his drinking habits and learn to live happily and usefully without alcohol. There, in association with others like himself, he can pour his problems in the ears of the sympathetic, tolerant, and understanding Charles Durfee and take part in a re-educational program which is not standardized but based upon the physical and psychological needs of the individual.

We have stressed Dr. Durfee's findings and therapy because we believe them to be more successful than that of the conventional psychoanalytical approach, which probes the patient's subconscious for the offending "psychological conditioning" that supposedly produces the neurosis giving rise to alcoholism—the mere symptom of that deep-seated trouble.

Alcoholics Anonymous was founded in Akron, Ohio, in 1934 by two alcoholics, one of them a Wall Street broker and the other an Ohio surgeon. Despite its disclaimer of any religious motive, Alcoholics Anonymous ranks with the Red Cross and the Salvation Army as one of the three most successful movements in applied Christianity of modern times. It had its origin in a theophany experienced by its agnostic cofounder, who is known affectionately to thousands as "Bill."

"He was sitting one evening at a kitchen table with a friend he knew as a life-long fellow-alcoholic. He offered this man a drink and was turned down. He was startled. His friend explained that he had joined a religious group which had taught him to believe in God, and he had thereby found the will-power to resist liquor. [Bill] was dumbfounded. For a month he continued to drink and to meditate upon this startling phenomenon. Then he went to a hospital to . . . have the whiskey sweated out of him. Finally, his head was clear. But his spirits were low. He decided to try to do what his friend had done. He concentrated on this thought, 'If there be a God, let Him show himself.'

"The result was instantaneous and incredible. There was a blinding, electric flash of white light. He seemed to be on a high mountain with a great wind of electric force blowing not only over him but through him. His body trembled with a consuming ecstasy, and a voice spoke these words, 'You are a free man.' The ecstasy subsided and he felt a great peace.

"He telephoned his hospital doctor, described his experience and asked him, 'Do you think I'm mad?'

"We don't know what the doctor really thought, but his answer was, 'No.' " [11]

Science doesn't know whether the recorded theophanies of history—experienced by Moses, Zoroaster, Gautama, Jesus, Paul, and many lesser men—were objective events or subjective experiences induced by the long periods of fasting that in each case preceded them. It doesn't really matter. Each was the prelude to a movement for human betterment. Bill's was no exception. A few months later he and his doctor friend founded Alcoholics Anonymous. In 1937 there were fifteen members. In July, 1950, there were ninety thousand, and they are acquiring twenty thousand new members each year. At the present writing, 50 per cent of the members in the four hundred groups in the United States, Canada, and overseas have not experienced a single relapse, while 25 per cent have

[145]

had only one or two "slips" or "slide-backs." The remaining 25 per cent have stumbled out of the ranks of sobriety more than three times, but the vast majority are still struggling to keep up with the band wagon.

What is the secret of this enormous success? Not all these men and women have had theophanies. Most of them have never even heard of their founder's experience. (To our knowledge this experience has been published only twice before.)

These are the elements of which that success is built: Alcoholics Anonymous is not tied to either the physiological or the psychological "school" of causation. In the opinion of the late Dr. William Duncan Silkworth, once Physician-in-Charge of the A. A. Wing in Knickerbocker Hospital, New York City, alcoholism is due primarily to a "physical allergy" but also to a "mental obsession." Alcoholics Anonymous is composed entirely of alcoholics who refer to themselves as such whenever they introduce themselves at an A. A. meeting. This gives the newcomer a measure of sympathetic understanding without censure or coddling that he could not possibly obtain from anyone but another alcoholic, who knows from personal experience everything he is undergoing.

He is given Twelve Steps to study and to practice. Printed on a small card to be carried in his pocket, they are the blueprint of a way of life which is essentially Christian. Indeed, religious scholars will find them reminiscent of *The Spiritual Exercises of Saint Ignatius Loyola*. But, of course, neither the Wall Street broker nor the Ohio doctor, who together wrote the Twelve Steps, could conceivably have read *The Exercises*. These are the Twelve Steps:

1. We admitted we were powerless over alcohol—that our lives had become unmanageable.
2. Came to believe that a Power greater than ourselves could restore us to sanity.

3. Made a decision to turn our will and our lives over to the care of God *as we understand Him.*

4. Made a searching and fearless moral inventory of ourselves.

5. Admitted to God, to ourselves, and to another human being the exact nature of our wrongs.

6. Were entirely ready to have God remove all these defects of character.

7. Humbly asked Him to remove our shortcomings.

8. Made a list of all persons we had harmed, and became willing to make amends to them all.

9. Made direct amends to such people whenever possible, except when to do so would injure them or others.

10. Continued to take personal inventory and when we were wrong promptly admitted it.

11. Sought through prayer and meditation to improve our conscious contact with God *as we understood Him* praying only for knowledge of His will for us and the power to carry that out.

12. Having had a spiritual awakening as a result of these steps we tried to carry this message to alcoholics, and to practice these principles in all our affairs.

In the twelfth step the new Alcoholics Anonymous member becomes the guide, sponsor, and counselor of a newer A. A. member. So the good work is carried forward in an ever-widening circle.

What A. A. has put into successful practice is essentially a cure by *faith,* similar to the many individual cases to which the late Dr. Alexis Carrel testified, to the astonishment of his medical colleagues. Science is baffled by the cure by faith, the occurrence of which it can neither deny nor adequately explain. Inasmuch as Alcoholics Anonymous is practicing this strange phenomenon upon a mass basis, it should afford some inquiring and not too bigoted minds an opportunity to elicit a rational explanation.

"There is another respect in which the work of Alcoholics

Anonymous on behalf of the alcoholic stands apart from that of most other agencies. It gives the middle-class drunk a break which he has long badly needed. In every large city hospital there is an alcoholic ward that saves the lives of and gives temporary rehabilitation to those alkys who were born in or who have sunk to the lowest strata of society. In various parts of the country there are exclusive sanatoria where, in a country-club-like atmosphere, the rich inebriate can sober up and try to make a fresh start. Until the advent of Alcoholics Anonymous the middle-class, that is, the average medium-income-bracket alcoholic, had no adequate curative agency suitable to his means and social position. . . .

"Speakers in Alcoholics Anonymous generally preface their remarks with the statement that the ideas they are about to express are their own and do not necessarily represent the views of the group as a whole. . . .

"It is one of the virtues of Alcoholics Anonymous that by means of this fluid type of organization it has escaped the evils of institutionalism so often inimical to movements for social betterment." [12]

The allergic basis for the physiological explanation of alcoholism is not by any means uniquely held by the medical advisers of Alcoholics Anonymous. But the exponents of this view admit that whatever may be behind the allergy is understood no more than any other allergy. In explaining the matter Dr. Silkworth said, "It would seem that through some defect, *probably in the metabolism* [italics are ours] . . ."

An echo of these words may be found in C. Lester Walker's *Harper's* article already quoted. "Professor Roger J. Williams, Director of the Biochemical Institute at the University of Texas, is a leading exponent of this idea [the metabolic]. He pointed out how often our metabolism differs from person to person in actual operating detail."

Last year William L. Laurence, science reporter of *The*

[148]

New York Times reported on the work being done by two different medical groups in New York City. He calls it "the glandular treatment for alcoholism [which] was first reported on over a year ago by Dr. John W. Tintera, chief of the Endocrine Clinic, St. John's Riverside Hospital, Yonkers, New York, and Dr. Harold W. Lovell of the New York Hospital and New York Medical College before the annual meeting of the American Geriatrics Society at Atlantic City." A more recent report —May, 1950—was made to the annual meeting of the Medical Society of the State of New York by Dr. James J. Smith, director of Research on Alcoholism at the New York University–Bellevue Medical Center. Both groups working independently, as often happens, had arrived at almost identical conclusions.

Alcoholism is caused by a deficiency in the adrenal cortical hormones—those hormones whose action is antithetical to insulin. The trouble may not be in the adrenal cortical itself, however, but in the master gland, the pituitary, which for some reason fails to stimulate the adrenal cortical glands as it does in normal operation of the endocrine system. It is believed, moreover, that this disability of the pituitary is not caused by the alcoholism but antedates its development. What is certain is that injections of ACTH, ACE, and cortisone have had a miraculous effect on drunks, even at their very worst, sobering them up with practically no hang-over within twenty-four hours of administration.[13]

These spectacular "cures" are a great step forward, and they provide evidence in reverse for the theory which the medical and the lay members of this collaboration arrived at independently: that hyperinsulinism, with its chronic partial blood sugar starvation, is an essential underlying condition of alcoholism.

To the lay writer it was just a bright idea to be discussed with anyone who would listen, especially with the many who knew a great deal more about alcoholism than he. Naturally, he discussed it with the medical collaborator and immediately learned that the latter had been doing more than merely thinking about it.

Looking back over twenty years as a diabetes specialist, he could not recall a single case of a diabetic who was also an alcoholic. Could it be that like the allergies—hay fever, asthma, rheumatic fever, and peptic ulcer—alcoholism also was one of those strange ailments associated with the low blood sugar of hyperinsulinism? Many factors pointed to the possibility. The reader may recall that those seeking a physiological rather than a psychological cause for alcoholism have pondered the possibility of allergy and metabolic imbalance. He may be impressed (as we were) by the strange similarity of many of the symptoms of alcoholism in its hang-over stages and of hyperinsulinism in its most definite forms. He may wonder if the alcoholic's strange craving for a nonaddictive drug may not be a craving for sugar, developed because the immediate effect upon the body of a dose of alcohol is similar to that of a dose of pure sugar. Thus, the alcoholic, not realizing he is sugar-starved, takes this erroneous way to stifle the pangs of a desire whose true origins he does not understand. In the course of recent practice the medical collaborator confirmed this hypothesis by the results of the Glucose Tolerance Test on alcoholics who came to him.

J.M. is a highly successful New York lawyer. His quick mind and highly keyed personality give him a decided advantage over slower-witted adversaries. As a trial counsel in civil suits he has won fabulous verdicts. The less spectacular and, perhaps, more scholarly branches of the law are repugnant to his temperament. He leaves them to the *briefers*. He enjoys matching wits with opposing counsel in the arena of the courtroom.

One day he noticed that he was not up to his usual brilliance. He found himself overlooking opportunities to raise objections and make remarks that would influence the jurors. He could hardly wait for the noon recess. He needed "a shot in the arm" so very badly! Finally his unuttered prayer was answered. The court recessed for luncheon.

The lawyer rushed out of the courtroom to the nearest café and ordered a "double Scotch on the double." As soon as the potion had passed his lips, he began to feel a little better. He knew the grateful warmth would course through his body in a few minutes and this knowledge made him less tense. He ordered another drink and another and another, until he became almost paralyzed with drink. Naturally he could not go on with the case, which had to be adjourned because of "illness of counsel."

On another occasion he developed the "awful thirst" toward the end of the day. Fortunately his associates were able to avert a legal tragedy (for the client) by taking him to a steam bath where they kept him all night to "boil him out." The next day he was able to go on with the case.

Similar episodes occurred with increasing frequency. The story began to get around and his practice to fall off. Too many cases were lost because he went to pieces at the crucial time. He was still capable of handling a short case, but when the issues were involved and many witnesses had to be examined and cross-examined, he simply could not remain sober long enough to complete his work. Eventually he began to drink as soon as he got up in the morning. An ounce of milk furnishes 20 calories. An ounce of 100-proof whisky yields 100 calories. As his alcoholic consumption increased, he ate less of other foods. His life became a perpetual lost week end.

He tried Alcoholics Anonymous, but their methods would not succeed with a man of his skeptical and analytical mind. This is not said in disparagement of the very great work that A. A. does. There are some, however, to whom the appeal would seem "revivalist." This sophisticated and cerebrating lawyer could not bring himself to "hit the sawdust trail."

He went to psychiatrist after psychiatrist. He knew them all too well. He had put so many through his brilliant cross-examinations. He knew all the answers himself and could not be influenced by others. He had been using suggestion on jurors for so many years that he was immune to it. He even went so far as to try hypnosis, but his mind was not amenable. He could never subject his will to another's. He could never forget to think for himself.

Finally a Glucose Tolerance Test was made—not because there was any particular indication for it, but because all other tests in general use had been performed without shedding any light on his compulsion. The test revealed that he had hyperinsulinism.

It was felt that his "thirst" was a cry for nourishment from his sugar-starved body. The patient was given the diet. His doctor made no reference to stopping drink. In three days the patient noticed that he no longer craved alcohol as much as before. He still drank, but that almost mad desire which formerly had come over him suddenly was gone. He found now that he could "take it or leave it." After a while he realized that liquor was not doing anything for him. He no longer needed its "lift." Being a sensible man, he stopped liquor completely without any outside suggestion.

In retrospect, it is easy to understand why he drank. In the beginning he had generally fortified himself against a tough legal battle by drinking several cups of black coffee. Coffee does stimulate the brain and make quick thinking easier. But the coffee's repeated stimulation of his islands of Langerhans had made them so sensitive that his blood sugar was forced down a few hours later, and he had a sinking sensation that led him to crave some further stimulation. The timing of his "binges" lends credence to this explanation. After dietary treatment had normalized his oversensitized islands of Langerhans, he no longer felt this need for a drink. Of course, he could better have relieved those spells of "gone" feelings with something to eat, but like too many people he believed that alcohol is a stimulant. The first stiff drink he took made him feel well by robbing him of the awareness of his difficulties. How natural, then, that he should want another to complete the job of restoration of his faculties. He could hardly deny the desire for a third, and so the vicious circle was established. Whenever he needed a boost the whisky bottle was at hand. He did not have the knowledge of his own body to know that he was really hungry. And in order to sober up quickly after a "binge," he would drink prodigious quantities of black coffee, which only spurred on the underlying trouble.

Another case is that of a man of thirty who had learned to take a drink while on combat duty as a bombardier in World War II. On his last mission the two right engines were put out of commission and the plane limped back to base. When it landed, the landing gear stuck, and the engines were driven back into the cockpit, killing the pilot and severely injuring the bombardier. He was invalided out of the service, and it was several years before he overcame the horror of that final experience. His family was indulgent with him and did not raise any serious objection whenever he took a drink "to steady his nerves." Gradually his alcoholic consumption mounted. He ate less and consumed great amounts of coffee. He had "the shakes." His hand trembled as he poured out his morning libation. His family frantically urged him to give up drink, but they could do nothing with him. His liver became enlarged and it was feared that he might be developing cirrhosis of the liver.

One day, while he was visiting his parents, he suddenly went into a stupor. He had not been drinking at all that day. Examination revealed an odor of acetone on his breath. He was given an injection of glucose intravenously and he soon revived. A few days later his mother telephoned the physician that she had attempted to reach her son by telephone and that his failure to answer made her fear that he had again col-

[153]

lapsed. She went with the doctor to her son's apartment. They found him still conscious but so drowsy that he had left his office and come home to sleep. His mother thought he was drunk, but the doctor again noticed that the odor on his breath was not spiritous but due to acetone. He was roused and told to take a glass of milk every two hours until the next day, when a Glucose Tolerance Test was taken. The results are so significant that we give the curve:

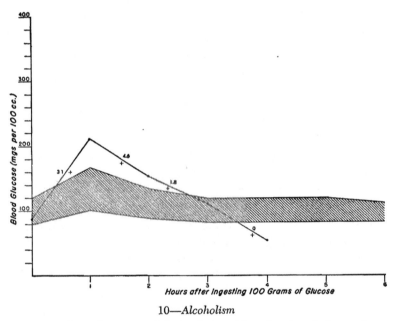

10—*Alcoholism*

This is obviously a case of dysinsulinism. The plus signs below each segment indicate that each urine specimen contained acetone. The test was terminated at the end of four hours because the patient went into insulin shock, the blood sugar being but 54 mg. per 100 cc.

At the fourth hour the patient had a convulsion, and glucose had to be administered intravenously. He was then told to take a small glass of milk every hour throughout the day and the following night.

This curve, at least for the first three hours, is a diabetic curve. The patient passed large amounts of sugar and acetone in his urine. If the test had not been prolonged the only possible diagnosis would have been diabetes—and of sufficient severity to require insulin. But the fourth-hour drop proved that it was a case of *dysinsulinism*. In all probability the liver had been so badly infiltrated with fat that its glycogen stores were depleted. Insulin would have done immeasurable harm. The patient had to be treated for his hyperinsulinism (ignoring the diabetic element) and treatment had to be given for the fatty liver, which now, fortunately, is not an impossible task. The young man was put on the Harris diet and, in addition, treated with large doses of vitamins and with lipotropic substances to aid in the regeneration of the liver. This was necessary because of the large amount of fat in the Harris diet. His urine was examined every day. For four days it was loaded with acetone and sugar. On the fifth day there was no more sugar, but there was still a slight amount of acetone, which persisted for another four days. His blood sugar was determined about an hour after luncheon. On the third day of treatment it was 176 mg. per 100 cc. of blood. On the fifth day it was 150, and on the seventh day, 138. On the tenth day of treatment it was down to only 100—and that only an hour after a heavy meal! The patient gained eleven pounds in the ten days. His appetite was enormous.

The young man was permitted to get out of bed. His family and friends came to see him and drinks were served. The next day he said that he was surprised that even while watching his guests drink, he did not have the slightest desire to join them.

At the time this account is being written, he is still under treatment. The enlarged liver has regressed to its normal size. He feels better than he has at any time since the end of the war. The vitamin injections have been cut down from daily to twice a week, but he is still taking the lipotropic capsules and is still on the Harris diet, except for the fortification of two glasses of milk with an ounce of brewer's yeast powder in each of them.

This young man's drinking was due to the let-down feelings induced by his drops in blood sugar. No amount of scolding or pleading could possibly influence him to stop. Only when the dips in blood sugar were eliminated was he able to resist the urge.

The temptation is strong to repeat the Glucose Tolerance Test to learn if the diabetic element has been removed. It would be foolish to do so, however, for it might upset the delicately balanced equilibrium and regenerate the entire process. We must be content with indirect evidence—the relatively low blood sugar and the urine's freedom from sugar and acetone—to assure us that the diabetes has been removed.

A dozen other cases were treated in the same manner as the first of these two cases. The results were uniformly good, and thus would seem to indicate that in alcoholism, as in the other allergies, hyperinsulinism is a necessary underlying condition. This conclusion does not run counter to the results obtained and the treatment given by Drs. Smith and Tintera with ACE and ACTH. On the contrary, as we shall show in the next chapter, these results are simply on opposite pans of the scales of endocrine balance.

7

The
Glandular Jazz Band

THE ENDOCRINE SYSTEM—THE ANTERIOR
PITUITARY—THE ADRENAL CORTEX—
CORTISONE AND ACTH—PREGNANCY

IF EACH MINUTE portion of the complex phenomenon we call life acted independently, it would make matters so much more easily understandable. Mother Nature, however, is not limited by the capacities of the human mind. Since we are unable to grasp more than a few variables at a time, we often must discuss different factors individually. Biological relationships are not so circumscribed. Any and all possible changes can take place simultaneously, so that there is a continuously shifting equilibrium between forces. If we recognize this multifaceted complexion of life, we do not fall into the errors of the various faddists and cultists who ascribe all human ills to this or that cause.

Because of just such complexity, we have held out on you. Now we shall fill in the gaps.

As the level of blood sugar changes, there is a shift in the concentrations of many other substances in the blood. For our purposes we may confine ourselves largely to the calcium (lime) in the blood. The human body harbors a considerable amount of calcium, more than 99 per cent of which is in the skeleton. The bones of a one hundred and fifty-pound man contain somewhat more than two and a half pounds of calcium, while his blood contains less than five grains. Yet this tiny amount of calcium is so important that he could not live without it.

⁄ Each 100-cubic-centimeter portion of blood contains between 10 and 11 milligrams of calcium. The amount in the blood *cells* is negligible, some investigators even reporting that there is none. When blood is taken from a vein for analysis, a little potassium oxalate or sodium citrate is added to remove the calcium, and thus prevent the blood from clotting. The blood remains fluid, permitting measurement for analysis. If calcium is to be determined, however, blood samples cannot be treated in this manner. The blood must be allowed to clot, and the calcium then determined in the clear fluid—the serum.

The calcium in blood serves other functions. Some of it is combined with the proteins (albumin and globulin) of the blood. Some of it exists in the same form as in any solution of a calcium salt. This so-called ionic calcium is of the utmost importance in maintaining a smooth action of the nervous system. When it is too low, we have a condition known as *tetany,* in which the muscles tend to go into spastic contractions.

The electron microscope, which can magnify so many more times than its optical predecessor, has revealed that each cell in the central nervous system has a shell of some calcium compound just within the outer wall.[1] When the integrity of this shell is impaired, the cell becomes too irritable.[2] This might be compared to the rubber insulation on the terminals in a telephone exchange. If that insulation breaks down, there is a spread of the electrical impulse, so that when we wish to call a particular number, we find ourselves on a perpetual party line. In a more or less similar manner, when the calcium shell is thinned out, the nervous impulses are not channelized

[158]

properly and we experience a spread of effect beyond the desired path.

Changes in the level of the sugar of the blood are reflected in shifts in the salts in the blood. Calcium, in particular, varies directly as the sugar. Fabrykant and Pacella demonstrated that hyperinsulinism is accompanied by low serum calcium values.[3] These same investigators also showed that these changes in sugar and calcium are accompanied by definite changes in the electroencephalogram—the recording of the electrical changes that continually occur in the brain. It should be remembered that the brain differs from all other tissue in being nourished solely by sugar. Hence, it is readily understandable how low blood sugar can have such a deleterious effect on our minds.

In treating any of the myriad manifestations of hyperinsulinism, we are not forced to give special consideration to the serum calcium deficiency. The diet will, in time, correct the condition by itself, and the serum calcium will rise along with the blood sugar. If we administer calcium with the diet, however, the process of recovery is accelerated, so that what would take months in the absence of calcium therapy takes but a few weeks.[4] This applies especially to hay fever.

There are other mineral constituents of the blood which vary somewhat with changes in the blood sugar level. Their effects are relatively unimportant, however, and need be mentioned only briefly. Among these minerals are sodium and potassium. The blood serum contains much more sodium than potassium, while the cells contain more potassium than sodium. The serum potassium is of some interest because it varies inversely with the levels of the blood sugar and serum calcium. Because sodium is antagonistic to potassium, it is advisable for persons with any of the different manifestations of hyperinsulinism to avoid excessive use of salt (sodium chloride). Asthmatics, it will be remembered, suffer much more with excessive use of salt. Therapeutically, we are not too concerned with serum potassium in hyperinsulinism but it is of considerable theoretical importance.

For even the most elementary understanding of the sugar problem, we must consider not only the islands of Langerhans but also many other endocrine glands. These organs, it will be remembered, appear to be clearly glandular in structure but lack any duct to carry their secretions to the point of application. Hence, they are called ductless glands, or glands of internal secretion. Their juices are picked up by the blood and carried to the areas where they are needed and used, a necessary mechanism because their effects are felt throughout the body.

The endocrine system has been aptly likened to a jazz band, with the pituitary gland as its leader. In the jazz band the leader may play one or more instruments, and the players generally follow his direction, but they are, to some extent, on their own—especially when they "get hot."

Weight for weight, the pituitary gland is the most important tissue in the body. In spite of its small size, being smaller than the end section of the little finger and weighing about half a gram ($\frac{1}{60}$ ounce), it exerts influences that profoundly affect and regulate almost all vital processes. Its importance is indicated by its protected location—at about the geometrical center of the brain—where it is sheltered in a cavity in the bone forming the roof of the nose and mouth. This space is called the *Sella Turcica* (Turkish saddle) from its fancied resemblance to that equestrian device.

The pituitary is divided into anterior and posterior parts which are readily separable. The anterior lobe of the pituitary has many important physiological functions, and commercially prepared extracts are available which can fulfill a single function to the almost complete exclusion of the others. These include:

[160]

1. The growth hormone, which controls normal growth. When present in excess during the period of growth, a person may attain a height of seven or eight feet. If present in insufficient amount, the result is a midget (the normally proportioned type). If the latter condition is recognized in its early stages, administration of the growth hormone will induce practically normal growing.

2. The adrenotropic hormone (ACTH), which stimulates the activity of the adrenal cortex. We shall discuss this more fully later on.

3. Gonadotropic hormones, two in number. One, the follicle-stimulating hormone, induces ovulation in the female and sperm formation in the male. It has been used in both sexes to correct retarded sexual development, and will induce menstruation in indicated cases. It can also be used in cases of undescended testicles to cause them to descend from the abdomen into the scrotum. The other, the luteinizing hormone, enables the gravid uterus to retain the pregnancy, and it has been used frequently to avert a threatened miscarriage. During pregnancy the urine contains enormous amounts of what is called APL (Anterior Pituitary-Like hormone); commercially, this is made from pregnant mares' urine. Its usage has been similar to that of the hormones extracted from the pituitary, and it also finds extensive application in preventing the hot flashes of the menopause.

4. The thyrotropic hormone stimulates thyroid activity and has been used in certain cases of hypothyroidism which appeared to be the secondary result of primary pituitary insufficiency.

Prolactin was also made from the anterior pituitary. It would start milk formation in mothers who were unable to nurse their infants. It has since been withdrawn from the market.

The anterior pituitary is antagonistic to the islands of Lan-

[161]

gerhans. It may be that this is an effect of ACTH, the adreno-tropic hormone, but the final answer must await further investigation.

If the anterior pituitary lobe becomes enlarged and over-active after the attainment of maturity, the growth of the body is no longer symmetrical. Certain parts grow enormously. The hands and feet and the lower jaw expand completely out of proportion to the rest of the body. This condition is known as *acromegaly*. The end result is an exaggeration of a Primo Carnera whose huge size is evidence of pituitary overactivity. Most acromegalics have diabetes, because the insulin apparatus is depressed by the excessive production of the anti-insulin anterior pituitary hormone. Acromegaly is characterized by periods of activity until, for some unknown reason, the process apparently comes to a halt. The diabetes then becomes milder, or may even disappear completely, as the excessive production of the anti-insulin factor ceases. With an exacerbation of the acromegaly, as indicated by another spurt in growth of the affected parts, the diabetes becomes more severe.

Some patients undergo many alternating phases. This condition occurs as a result of the nonselective quality of the enlarged pituitary, in which all the hormones, rather than a particular one, are made more plentiful.

The anti-insulin effect of the anterior pituitary is also illustrated by the researches of Houssay, of Buenos Aires.[5] He demonstrated that removal of the anterior pituitary increased the sensitivity to insulin in otherwise normal animals. In other words, a smaller dose of insulin sufficed to produce the same drop in blood sugar that was obtained in an intact animal. If the pancreas had been removed previously, the diabetes caused by the extirpation of the islands of Langerhans was rendered less severe when the anterior pituitary was removed. When an extract of the anterior pituitary was injected into normal animals, the subsequent injection of insulin had less effect than it had before the injection of the pituitary extract. If the anterior pituitary was first removed and then the pancreas was extirpated, the animal rarely developed diabetes, and then of merely a trivial nature. When these Houssay animals, as they have been called, were injected with pituitary extract, they developed diabetes or, if they already had that condition in a mild form, it became extremely severe, similar to the normal animals whose pancreases alone had been removed. Permanent diabetes has been produced in animals by repeated injection of pituitary extracts.[6] If the injections are stopped before the islands of Langerhans are permanently damaged, however, the diabetes disappears. If, finally, the pituitary extract is injected together with insulin, diabetes is not produced.[7]

The posterior lobe of the pituitary secretes what was formerly believed to be a single hormone, pituitrin, which is manufactured from the pituitary glands of cattle. It has been used successfully for the treatment of *diabetes insipidus*. It will be remembered that this disease is quite different from diabetes mellitus. The urine contains no sugar, and the blood sugar is normal. The victim of this disease passes gallons of pale, watery urine each day. If he inhales pituitary powder or takes injections of pituitary solution, he can control his disease —but not cure it.

Pituitrin is also used very widely in surgery and obstetrics. Sometimes, after an operation, for example, there is paralysis of the bowel. This "post-operative ileus" is treated by injecting pituitrin, which stimulates the smooth (involuntary) muscle coats of the intestines, causing them to contract and expel their contents. Having a similar muscular coat, the walls of blood vessels will contract upon pituitrin injection, causing the blood pressure to rise. In obstetrics, pituitrin is injected into the new mother after delivery of the infant to shrink the uterus. It has been found that these two functions —surgical and obstetrical—are performed by two different fractions of pituitrin: *pitressin*, which affects the bowels and blood vessels, and *pitocin*, which affects the uterus. These are now available separately.

The thyroid gland also influences the blood sugar. In cases of overactivity of the thyroid gland, there is a tendency for the blood sugar to rise. If hyperthyroidism is engrafted on an already existing diabetes, the latter condition becomes much more severe. Surgical removal of the thyroid will then alleviate the diabetes.

The body is a remarkable complexity of checks and balances. If the biceps muscle is tightened, for example, the forearm will not move—the opposing triceps muscle must also be released. The positions of our members depend upon the equilibrium between the flexing and extending muscles around the various joints. The central nervous system is somewhat like a factory's wiring system, which controls the actions of the different machines and carries information about their workings to the main office. The central nervous system can be divided into the voluntary and involuntary nervous systems. The former controls our muscles of locomotion as well as the sensory region which brings impressions to our consciousness. The involuntary, or autonomic, system controls the vegetative functions of the body not directly under the control of the will, although automatic adjustments of these bodily functions that take place without our awareness may be induced by voluntary motions. This autonomic nervous system is divided functionally into the sympathetic and parasympathetic systems. The latter is also called the vagus system, from its principal nerve, the vagus. These two parts are antagonistic in their actions. For example, the sympathetic nerves quicken the pulse, raise the blood pressure, and slow the movements of the intestinal tract, while the vagus has opposite effects.[8] The most notable drug that stimulates the sympathetic system is adrenalin, the secretion of the central portion of the adrenal glands. The animal can live indefinitely

[164]

without the adrenal medullas. Apparently, adrenalin is used by the body only for emergencies. When the animal is in danger and must be prepared for "fight or flight," adrenalin pours into the blood. The heart quickens; the blood pressure rises as the visceral blood vessels contract; intestinal movements are slowed down; and the liver converts some of its insoluble glycogen into soluble glucose, causing the blood sugar to rise. These actions furnish more and richer blood to the skeletal muscles so that the whole organism is alerted to combat the peril.

Under ordinary circumstances the adrenal cortex (the outer portions of the glands), without which we cannot live, supplies the cortical hormones to the blood. The cortical hormones act very much the same as adrenalin but with far less intensity. They also have other actions, vital to good health, which we shall discuss in due course. Insofar as blood sugar concentration is concerned, the level is maintained by the interplay of the cortical hormones and insulin. The former tend to raise the blood sugar level by causing the liver to change some of its glycogen into glucose, which is then dissolved in the blood leaving the liver. This process has been given the formidable name of *glycogenolysis* or *gluconeogenesis*. The secretion of the cortical hormones is stimulated by a fall in blood sugar as it is consumed by our bodies' activities. The subsequent rise in blood sugar removes this stimulus by inducing the islands of Langerhans to produce insulin which in turn enables the liver to withdraw glucose from the blood and store it in the form of insoluble glycogen against future demand. When we drive an automobile along a straight road, we do not hold the car to a perfectly straight course. We weave from side to side, correcting our departures from the course by appropriate turns of the steering wheel. The seasoned driver is distinguished from the novice by the size of these swings. Similarly, a well-adjusted and conditioned organism will deviate only slightly from the optimum level of

[165]

blood sugar. In the poorly functioning organism, the swings are much greater.

If we wish to correct an imbalance in the involuntary nervous system, we can either depress the overactive part or stimulate the underactive part. We have drugs that can fulfill these functions. Sometimes it is advisable to stimulate one system and depress the opposing one by the simultaneous administration of two drugs.

There is a disease of the adrenal cortex called Addison's disease, in which there is a deficiency of a cortical hormone —cortin. This fortunately rare affliction, which only until recently was invariably fatal, is characterized by extremely low blood sugar levels. The blood pressure is very low, salt is lost from the body, and there is marked dehydration. The muscles are exceedingly weak and there is great emaciation, far beyond that accounted for by the loss of water. The victim exhibits a peculiar dark pigmentation of the skin and mucous membranes, especially around the body orifices. Patients were helped somewhat by being fed large amounts of salt which enabled them to retain more water, but this measure only slightly delayed the inevitable death. With the discovery of cortin, this dreadful process was prevented.[9] The symptoms of this disease resemble somewhat those of hyperinsulinism, but Addison's disease is, of course, much more serious and severe.

During the past twenty years there has been accelerated interest in the hormones of the adrenal glands. For some time it was thought that adrenalin was the only secretion, but, when it was shown that adrenalin came only from the medulla, the cortex was thoroughly investigated in many laboratories. Kendall,* working at the Mayo Clinic laboratories, isolated six crystalline substances from the adrenal cortex.[10] These were designated by the names, Compounds A, B,

* Dr. Edward C. Kendall, who retired from the Mayo Foundation on May 1, 1951.

C, D, E, and F, respectively. They are all related chemically, and it is quite possible that they represent stages in the manufacture of the hormone from other substances. As far back as 1930 it was found that Compound E had an effect on blood sugar antagonistic to insulin.

In animal experiments it was demonstrated that removal of the adrenal glands after the pancreas had been extirpated reduced the severity of the artificial diabetes.[11] When cortical extracts were administered to these animals, the diabetes again became severe.[12] If these cortical extracts were injected into normal animals, the blood sugar rose.[13] This parallels Houssay's experiments with the pituitary gland.

Because the tiny adrenal cortex could not supply these substances in quantity, attempts were made to prepare them chemically from more plentiful sources. Reichstein prepared a substance similar to Kendall's Compound E.[14] Kendall himself succeeded in preparing Compound A from desoxycholic acid, which is found in bile.[15] Sarett then devised a fairly efficient method to convert Compound A into Compound E,[16] and the commercial manufacture of Compound E finally was begun.

The successful preparation of Compound E made front-page copy, and the patent medicine men went into operation. A substance in wheat germ oil, called *vitamin* E, has one definitely proven effect: without it rats are sterile. No other effects of vitamin E have been definitely demonstrated, although it has been peddled for various conditions on which it has no effect. After the press published the startling accounts of the effectiveness of *Compound* E for certain conditions, the sales of *vitamin* E (which in no way is connected with Compound E) rose sharply. One company advertised "Vitamin E Compound."[17] To protect the public from such advertising, Kendall coined the name "cortisone," which he derived by combining some of the letters in its chemical name, 11-dehydro-17-hydroxyCORTICOsteroNE.[18]

[167]

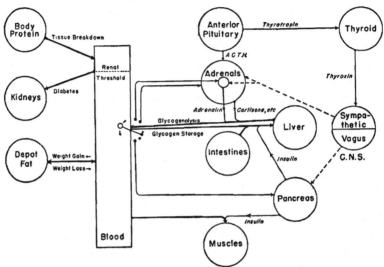

11—The Principal Influences on the Blood Sugar Level

This schematic diagram shows the principal hormonal, metabolic, and nervous mechanisms which regulate the level of the glucose in the blood. The fine lines indicate hormonal effects and the direction of the influence. The heavy lines indicate movements of glucose. The broken lines indicate effects from and on the sympathetic and parasympathetic (vagus) nervous systems. The hormones are represented in italics.

The small float indicates the effect of changes in the blood sugar level. When the float rises, the pancreas is stimulated to secrete insulin; when it falls, the adrenal cortical hormones are secreted. A rapid or profound fall also stimulates the production of adrenalin. These hormonal effects then tend to restore the blood sugar level to its optimal value. In addition to its nutritive action, glucose, in a way, thus acts as a hormone.

When enough of the new material was available, Hench and his assistants at the Mayo Clinic tried it in treating rheumatoid arthritis, a crippling condition in which the joints are swollen, tender, stiff, and painful to pressure. In addition, the muscles pulling on the affected joints tend to go into spasm, jamming the sore joint still tighter, and the muscles themselves ache unbearably with the cramp of their unrelieved contractions. Almost every train arriving in Arizona

[168]

disgorges its quota of victims of this distressing malady; sufferers are less uncomfortable in dry climates.

Dr. Hench noticed that people with rheumatoid arthritis were frequently relieved of their pain when they had attacks of jaundice, while women sufferers were quite comfortable during pregnancy.[19] This led him to believe that the condition was not wholly irreversible.

/The pituitary hormones build up in the blood of pregnant women. This is the basis for the commercial isolation of the sex factors from pregnancy urine, since the large excess spills over into the urine. Dr. Louis Granirer recently demonstrated that arthritics can be benefited by injecting them with plasma made from blood that has been drawn from women forty-eight hours after childbirth.[20] This was in line with Hench's observations.

Gold salts have been used with varying success in the treatment of rheumatoid arthritis. This occasional efficacy might well be explained on the grounds of some toxic effect on the liver, for when gold compounds are given to the point of intoxication, jaundice is a most prominent symptom—again commensurate with Hench's observations.

In 1949 Hench treated several patients who had rheumatoid arthritis by injecting them with cortisone. Within a few days the stiffness of their joints disappeared. The pain was relieved and, in the course of a week or so, the swelling diminished. There is a laboratory test used in the diagnosis of rheumatoid arthritis, in which the blood is treated to prevent clotting and then placed in a narrow-bored tube. The corpuscles, being heavier than the plasma, settle in the tube. In normal persons they will settle somewhat less than 20 millimeters in an hour. In rheumatoid arthritics the sedimentation rate is several times as rapid. In the cases treated with cortisone, the sedimentation rate became normal in a few weeks. The muscle spasm disappeared, but the anatomical changes in the bones and joints were not affected.

It has been known that cases of rheumatoid arthritis sometimes have periods of spontaneous remission. The patients Hench and Kendall treated felt so much better subjectively that these investigators feared the effect might have been purely psychic. Without informing the patients, they substituted sterile salt water for the cortisone. The symptoms returned within a few days. When treatment was resumed with the drug, the patients' symptoms again disappeared. This proved that the hormone actually had the anticipated effect. In treatment, the drug must be given indefinitely, since the symptoms return on its withdrawal.[21]

The cortisone treatment was uniformly successful, and it earned for the discoverers the 1950 Nobel Prize in medicine, which they shared with Reichstein. The same treatment was tried in cases of acute rheumatic fever which appears to be aborted by the drug,[22] but the investigators, with admirable scientific restraint, do not as yet claim that this treatment should supersede the older therapy with salicylates.

Unfortunately the use of this drug is not unattended by serious danger. In most of the conditions for which it has been used, there is no clear evidence of adrenal hormone deficiency. Therefore, in treating with cortisone (or with ACTH, which causes the patient's own adrenal glands to secrete more of their hormones) we produce an excess of such adrenal hormone secretions—*hyperadrenalism* of at least a mild degree.

There is a rare disease of the adrenal glands, Cushing's disease, in which the patient exhibits rather bizarre signs. The face becomes round; the hair on the face and body increases (in both sexes); acne is commonly produced; a lump of firm fat grows on the back of the neck (the so-called buffalo hump); fat is deposited around the hips; and there is increased pigmentation of the skin. The female patient may stop menstruating. There may be a diabetic condition. Potassium is lost from the blood and sodium is retained. There may be

[170]

high blood pressure. Any or all of these symptoms may be produced either by excessive use of cortisone or ACTH or by their administration to a hypersensitive patient.

In addition to these dangers, cortisone and ACTH have produced excessive coagulability of the blood so that clots may form within the blood vessels, i.e., thrombosis. An occasional patient has been rendered psychotic, and many of them are "euphoric"—they feel a happiness to which their state of health does not entitle them. This euphoria, curiously enough, occurs in the final stages of tuberculosis, and has long been known as the herald of approaching death.

Fortunately, most of these untoward symptoms disappear promptly on withdrawal of the drug. Occasionally, however, the changes are permanent.

Since ACTH is made from the pituitary gland, it is almost impossible to keep all of the posterior pituitary out of the extract. Some sensitive people have experienced transient episodes of extremely high blood pressure following each injection. They have suffered severe abdominal cramps. In a few cases the blood pressure has risen so precipitously that hemorrhages have occurred within the skull.

Consequently it would be foolhardy indeed to administer these powerful drugs to those whose conditions already indicate an inherent danger. Neither cortisone nor ACTH should be given to persons suffering from diabetes or high blood pressure (hypertension). Those who have experienced psychotic episodes should be denied these drugs, as well as those who have had indications of any condition associated with blood clots. Persons with heart trouble should not take them, because of their sodium-retentive quality, which might induce heart failure.

There is another effect of hyperadrenalism that might prove dangerous: infection may occur without attendant fever (which warns of infection). For this reason the American Trudeau Society placed warnings in the press (December

[171]

4, 1950), advising that cortisone and ACTH not be used for tuberculosis and that arthritics be examined for latent tuberculosis before being treated with the drugs.

A potential danger discovered only recently lies in the tendency of both drugs to raise the serum cholesterol.[23] Since high cholesterol levels probably induce arteriosclerosis (opinion still is divided), one must reserve judgment as to the safety of the drugs when used over a long period. While the blood cholesterol tends to decline *toward* its initial value after the drug is withheld for a time, it is possible that a dangerous process may have been initiated.

These several considerations demonstrate the antagonism between the adrenal cortex and the islands of Langerhans. The resultant drop in serum potassium has been recognized only recently as a dangerous condition. It can cause muscle weakness, muscular irritability (manifested by twitchings), and often paralysis of muscles and changes in the heart.[24] The muscle weakness first affects the trunk and limbs, while in some cases the muscles of respiration are paralyzed, resulting in death. When affected, the heart muscle becomes flabby and the beat is more feeble and rapid, while there are characteristic changes in the electrocardiogram.

The bromidic statement that "support creates the need for support" is frequently valid, as, for example, in the use of cortisone. When the natural secretion of cortisone is replaced or supplemented by externally administered doses, the demand on the adrenal glands decreases. Consequently, when the drug is withdrawn, the glands may have reached a state of inactivity which in turn may result in a case of *hypo*adrenalism.

Another objection to the use of cortisone stems from our uncertainty as to its being the *only* secretion of the cortex. There is good reason to believe that the cortex secretes at least two and probably three hormones. Administration of cortisone results in the circulation of that hormone alone. For this reason many clinicians prefer ACTH to cortisone, because ACTH stimulates the adrenal glands to produce more of its own hormones. These hormones then are released into the circulation in approximately their proper proportions. In excess, however, ACTH can produce the same ill effects as cortisone overdosage.

In reconsidering the Houssay experiments, it will be remembered that the depancreatized animal failed to develop diabetes with the removal of the pituitary. The phenomenon usually is ascribed to the removal of the pituitary itself. It would appear possible, however, that diabetes failed to occur because the removal of the pituitary in turn *removed the stimulus to the adrenal glands*—which would have caused diabetes in the absence of the insulin of the pancreas. While pure supposition, this concept is of considerable theoretical importance, because it coordinates many otherwise unrelated phenomena.

In addition to its application to rheumatoid arthritis and acute rheumatic fever, ACTH has been tried for almost every condition for which we have no effective remedy. While it has proved extremely effective in the treatment of bronchial asthma,[25] its results in other conditions are still too equivocal to reach a definite conclusion.

The symptoms of peptic ulcer as well as those of rheumatoid arthritis are temporarily alleviated during pregnancy.[26] This, it is believed, results from the large amount of anterior pituitary hormones secreted into the blood. Recently, however, ACTH and cortisone were tried in long-standing ulcer cases, but with disappointing results. The patients showed signs of impending perforation, and operations had to be performed.[27] This may have been caused by the known deleterious effect of these hormones on the blood vessels. The drugs were tried in a few patients and in a large number of experimental animals. All of the cases except one, however, were severe and of long duration. The milder case responded

[173]

quite well, but the patient soon had the side reactions (buffalo hump and moon face), so that the therapy was stopped. The ulcer symptoms then promptly returned. The therapy would have received a fairer trial with less severe cases.

The beneficent influence of pregnancy has its probable explanation in the glucose of the blood. The glucose tolerance curve, it will be remembered, tends to be higher during pregnancy. Because the large amounts of pituitary hormones circulating in the blood (as well as cortisone, which is increased by the stimulation of the adrenal cortex) are antagonistic to insulin, any excessive amount of insulin will be smothered. The blood glucose, therefore, will tend to be higher, and conditions in which low blood sugar levels are found will tend to become milder.

Burbank has noticed that arthritics have a tendency to low blood sugars, and the level tends to rise as they improve.[28]

With this hypothesis in mind, a patient with rheumatoid arthritis was subjected to the six-hour Glucose Tolerance Test. The result?

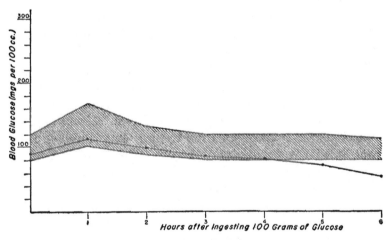

12—*Rheumatoid Arthritis*

This curve is typical for hyperinsulinism.

[174]

The patient had subclinical hyperinsulinism.

If there is any merit to this hypothesis, the very first case tested must give such a result, for this theory cannot be based on a statistical study. EVERY case must behave the same way. If this test had not indicated hyperinsulinism, the entire project would have been abandoned. Conclusions cannot be drawn from a single case, of course, and work to test the validity of our assumptions is now in progress. On its completion, it will be reported in a standard medical journal.[29] Naturally, we hope that we may be able to help arthritics along the same lines that have been so effective for the other conditions. The treatment for hyperinsulinism does not depend on any scarce and costly drug, and it has the further advantage of not requiring hospitalization. It would be wonderful if it succeeds. But at this writing it must remain in the lap of the gods.

In gout there is an impaired excretion of uric acid which piles up in the blood. Treatment with ACTH or cortisone increases the excretion enormously and the symptoms clear up rapidly. Withdrawal of either drug, however, is followed by another severe attack.[30] Gout is very rare in diabetics.[31]

The Glucose Tolerance Test was given to a man who had had many attacks of gout. The drop in blood sugar to 63 mg. per 100 cc. showed him to have hyperinsulinism. A complete investigation, however, would require the facilities of a hospital. This will be done.

8

Hyperinsulinism—
Key to Many Doors

SUBCLINICAL HYPERINSULINISM, CAUSE
OR EFFECT?—MORE CASE HISTORIES—
SUICIDE— MURDER— EPILEPSY— "CARES,
DIFFICULTIES, AND TROUBLES"—THE
GOLDEN KEY

WE HAVE INDICATED many bodily functions
which can be affected by hyperinsulinism. Our list may not
now be complete, and time undoubtedly will reveal other
ways in which low blood sugar is felt by the human organism.
The protean manifestations of hyperinsulinism are not difficult to understand. Since glucose is fuel for all bodily activities, chronic partial starvation of the entire body produces
difficulty in the operation of its parts. Each cell in the body is
affected to some degree. We assign the effect to some specific part or system of the body because of our unavoida-
bly limited comprehension of the problem. Nature, however,
does not suffer from the limitations of the human intellect,
which can grasp but a few factors at a time. Nature functions
in accordance with *all* its factors. Yet, while the entire human
machine may be affected, it is possible that we may be aware
of the misbehavior of only one or two parts.

For this reason piecemeal treatment of patients so often is

[176]

unsatisfactory. When one ailment of the body is corrected, the patient may then notice other organs which have been out of adjustment, symptoms which had been overshadowed. By nourishing all parts of the body at once, the entire being is brought into better adjustment. Treatment should be fundamental.

Often the question arises as to whether subclinical hyperinsulinism is the *cause* or the *effect* of accompanying illnesses. It does not make any difference. Such a cause-or-effect concept is grounded in the limitations of human reasoning. We like to imagine a well-ordered state of affairs in which each action is produced by some antecedent cause and in turn produces its own effect. But again, Nature does not function in this manner.

Assume we have a certain amount of any gas in a suitable container. Under specified conditions of temperature and pressure, it will occupy a definite volume. If we raise the temperature, the gas will expand to occupy more space, or, if we confine it in the same space, the pressure will rise. If we apply more pressure to the gas, it will contract its volume and it will get hotter. If we allow it to expand by releasing the pressure, it becomes colder. In all these changes we consider the change in pressure to be the cause of the changes in temperature and volume, or the change in temperature to be the cause of the changes in the remaining two, etc. Pressure, volume, and temperature are so interrelated that only certain combinations of them can exist for any given quantity of the gas.

Similarly, our concern as to whether hyperinsulinism is cause or effect is groundless. We should recognize the fact that while the body can function under all sorts of conditions, we are so constituted that it operates most efficiently under rather rigidly limited conditions. If we depart too much from the conditions to which we are adapted, our ease is impaired— we have dis-ease. If we can restore the optimum conditions

[177]

for the operation of the body, it will accommodate itself to the new set of circumstances and will function with greater ease. In all cases of undesirable functioning of the body accompanied by low blood sugar, the only condition of the body that is vulnerable to therapy of a simple nature is the level of the blood glucose. When we raise that level, the other factors adjust themselves to a new condition of equilibrium which we find more comfortable. So the dis-ease is eliminated. Of course, we can reach a satisfactory point of equilibrium by other means. We can administer ACTH or cortisone to counteract the excessive secretion of insulin. Or we can give drugs, such as the belladonna preparations which depress the activity of the parasympathetic nervous system, or those which stimulate the sympathetic nervous system (adrenalin, ephedrine, etc.), in an attempt to reach a satisfactory balance. We like our method—it requires no drugs. Occasionally the need for drugs is imperative but when withdrawn, the body must readjust to the new conditions imposed by the withdrawal. This second readjustment should not be applied to the body unless absolutely necessary. Most routine cases do not require drugs.

This account would not be complete without the inclusion of a few case histories to illustrate the application of the principles we have attempted to describe. Some of these cases may defy specific classification, because they include symptoms of several different ailments.

G.M.K. is a prominent photographer. For a number of years he had "felt bad" and had consulted more than a score of doctors. He had symptoms of ulcer of the stomach, but X-ray examination failed to confirm its presence. He suffered from "sinus trouble" and coughed severely each morning. He was deeply depressed and eventually found that his preoccupation with his symptoms interfered with his work. In 1948 he

[178]

reached the end of his endurance and made preparations to liquidate his business and retire to Arizona. Under fifty years of age, the patient was resigned to a life as a crochety dyspeptic. His symptoms, then, were gastric, allergic, and mental. The six-hour Glucose Tolerance Test revealed the only condition which could account for these variegated symptoms: hyperinsulinism. After only three weeks on the Harris diet, his symptoms gone, the patient dropped his plans to retire and now, four years later, is still actively engaged in his work.

B.W. is a housewife of forty-five. During her young adult life she had a toxic goiter which she tolerated for some twenty years because of fear of surgery. Her condition finally became so severe that she submitted to an operation and recovered. Soon, however, she began to gain weight and became terribly concerned about it. She thought she could stifle the pangs of hunger by drinking several cups of black coffee each day.

After a few months on this self-imposed diet she noticed that she suffered from vague intestinal complaints. At first these consisted of an occasional twinge of pain in the lower left side of the abdomen, but soon the attacks became more severe. Usually they occurred during the early hours of morning. She consulted a physician, who naturally ordered an X-ray study of her intestinal tract. His diagnosis was regional ileitis and he recommended an operation. The operative procedure is quite formidable, for it requires removing a few feet of the last part of the small intestine and connecting the remainder to the colon. The physician felt that the operation was urgent because by now the attacks occurred nightly, awakening the patient at about three or four o'clock in the morning in excruciating pain.

She consulted another physician who was aware of hyperinsulinism. He examined her X rays and found indication of spasm of the bowel and not regional ileitis. The X rays were then submitted to a roentgenologist of unquestioned eminence who agreed that there was nothing to suggest regional ileitis.

A six-hour Glucose Tolerance Test revealed hyperinsulinism, and B.W. was placed on the Harris diet. Her attacks stopped within a week and have not occurred for three years —without an operation!

To repeat a word of caution: if one wishes to take off weight by diet, coffee should be avoided, because the caffeine only temporarily stills the appetite by inducing a blood sugar increase. Soon the islands of Langerhans become sensitized, and once the insulin performs its function, the coffee's appetite-quenching qualities are most brief—and followed by a ravenous appetite!

P.J., a woman of forty-eight, had suffered from claustrophobia (among other things) for fifteen years. After a futile five-year search for relief from her "nervousness," she submitted to psychoanalysis—for two more years. Next she underwent a course of electric shock treatments, and for a year or so she was without complaint. Soon, however, her memory returned, and with it her old phobias, plus a few new ones as well. P.J. was exhausted. Life no longer was attractive, and she considered suicide. In desperation she tried another psychiatrist, and another, and yet another—all without success. Finally she yielded to family pressure and submitted to complete examination.

P.J. revealed that for years she had eaten but one meal a day, in the evening. Arising after the rest of her family had eaten, she simply could not bring herself to eat a solitary meal. To appease her hunger she drank prodigious amounts of strong tea.

Only one positive physical abnormality was found: the characteristic tenderness and protective muscular spasm in the left upper abdomen. The hyperinsulinism condition was confirmed by the Glucose Tolerance Test, in which the blood sugar dropped to 63 within five hours. With the blood sugar drop, P.J. felt faint; she reeled from the laboratory and wolfed down the usual postexamination glass of milk, following it with an enormous breakfast. After the meal she felt better, and the nature of her ailment was discussed. She interrupted the discourse with:

"Doctor, did you say that I make too much insulin?"

"Exactly. You have the opposite of diabetes."

"Then if I were given an injection of insulin, what would be the effect?"

"It would give you your usual symptoms with even greater severity." (As a matter of fact, a large enough dose might even prove fatal.)

"Well, three weeks ago the psychiatrist who was then treating me gave me two injections, and after each one I felt the same way I did right after the test you gave me today. I asked him what he had injected and he said he had given me small doses of insulin. After the second injection I felt so weak I could hardly go home, and I refused to continue the treatment. And he didn't give me any tests. He didn't even examine me!"

P.J. was given the usual treatment for hyperinsulinism. Within a week she began to feel better, both physically and emotionally. In two weeks she was able to travel alone, which had been impossible for years. Today her anxieties are gone. The improved somatic health has fortified her against anticipated mental strain.

M.H., a woman of thirty-six, complained of fatigue, "nervousness," and irritability. She could hardly attend to her household responsibilities, and she was always too tired to go out evenings with her husband. After several years of searching for health, the patient received a Glucose Tolerance Test. It was positive, and she was placed on the Harris diet, to which she responded quite well. She was amazed that she was not given any sedative medication; she had exhausted the collection of barbiturates which had been previously prescribed for her nervousness.

She complained, however, that she must have her morning coffee (three cups!), that she was "not fit to live with" unless she did. She was advised that she would feel better and be easier to live with if she gave up coffee. The patient did as she was told; she soon felt much better.

At each visit she would ask how soon she might drink coffee and was advised that she should never drink it. Moderate use of caffeine is perfectly harmless to the average person; once the insulin apparatus has been sensitized by overindul-gence, however, coffee must be avoided.

In a way, this is similar to the alcohol problem. Moderate use of alcohol is not only relatively harmless but actually of help in withstanding the stress of civilized life. If a person has been an alcoholic and conquered his craving, he must not take another drop.

M.H. had to learn the hard way! She decided that one cup of coffee would do no harm, and for a while it did not. In a few months, however, her symptoms returned—"butterflies" in the stomach, intestinal spasm, more nervousness. She returned to the diet for a few weeks, had a few calcium injections, and again all was well.

N.K. is a young World War II veteran. A survivor of the infamous Bataan death march, he was a prisoner of war for more than three years, during which time he was systematically starved and beaten. When rescued he weighed some ninety pounds; after several months' care in an army hospital he was discharged weighing about one hundred sixty pounds, his normal weight. He continued treatment, however, attending Veterans Administration clinics regularly. He complained of several varied symptoms. In addition to those understandably attributable to his digestive system, he was jumpy, and he suffered frequent nightmares in which he re-experienced his prison-camp beatings. He was referred to the neuropsychiatric department, where he was given a bottle of sedatives on each visit.

Eventually the patient was given the Glucose Tolerance Test, which revealed hyperinsulinism. In addition to the Harris diet, he was given a few injections of calcium to boost his low blood calcium. Within a few weeks he began to lose his nervousness, and the nightmares disappeared. To us it is obvious why he suffered the nightmares. During the night his blood sugar would drop, producing the sensation of hunger, and by association he would relive his terrible prison-camp experiences, in which he had always been hungry. Once the blood sugar drops were prevented, he no longer had the nightmares. Today he is well and vigorous in both mind and body.

A.B., a member of an internationally prominent family, came to America after undergoing the many vicissitudes of the chaotic war and postwar periods in Europe. She was extremely shy and retiring and refused to associate with any of the young men who tried to contact her. As a child she had had rheumatic fever, and during the previous five or six years she suffered from serious heart trouble. She was subject to severe attacks of tachycardia. In addition she was terrified by height; extreme effort was required for her to go above the third floor in any building.

Many investigations were conducted, but all failed to disclose the source of her condition. Inevitably she was advised that her condition was psychosomatic, that her physical difficulties were primarily the result of her emotional difficulties. While her physician refused to accept this theory, he still was unable to supply another any more valid. Finally A.B. came to Dr. Richard Hoffmann who, recognizing the possibility of hyperinsulinism, suggested she place herself in the care of his associated internist—the medical collaborator of this book. Investigation of her sugar metabolism corroborated Dr. Hoffmann's suspicion, and with the Harris diet A.B. fully recovered. Her physical symptoms disappeared. Her heart functions normally, except for one or two recurrences a year, when she treats herself by resuming the Harris diet for a week or two. A curious effect of the treatment was the complete cessation of her besetting fears. She has conquered her diffidence and has become interested in people. She is about to be married. And last year she reported spending an enjoyable summer vacation . . . mountain climbing!

S.M. is a woman of sixty-nine who had been troubled with numerous allergies for many years. She had a strong tendency toward hypochondria and had been seen by almost every prominent allergist. She had positive skin reactions to almost one hundred allergens. I (Dr. Abrahamson) saw her for the first time when, following the use of a "hormonal cream" at a beauty parlor, she had an allergic attack which caused her face to puff up. She was tested and found to have hyperinsulinism. After a few weeks on the Harris diet, her allergies disappeared. But then she began to backslide and to eat sweets without restriction. Within a few days her hands became puffy and itched severely. No external signs of irritation, such as spots or redness, were visible. She was given an injection of a calcium preparation and the puffiness was relieved overnight. She was warned again about eating sweets.

One day she ate some fish, with, as she put it, "fear and trepidation." She had almost always experienced severe itching and blotching of her skin a few hours after she ate fish. This time, however, nothing happened. She repeated the experiment with other varieties of fish, and with eggs, to which she was particularly sensitive. What happened? Nothing. Her allergies had completely disappeared. So long as she maintained her blood sugar level, *she could not have* ANY *allergies.*

There are some sixteen thousand suicides each year in the United States. We believe a great part of them to be preventable. Many—perhaps most—of those who take their own lives are victims of the profound depression and ultimately irresistible urge to escape from life that so often is a manifestation of severe functional hyperinsulinism. A few case histories may serve to substantiate this theory.

E.W. is a woman of forty-eight who is married to an indulgent, successful, retired businessman, twenty-five years her elder. Two years ago she became obsessed with the idea of having to go to work, both for financial security and to occupy the hours her husband spent at his club. She became morose and then greatly depressed. Her husband became ill and stopped most of his activities, spending his time sitting in a chair as a semi-invalid instead of at his club.

One night while she and her husband were talking E.W. suddenly slumped from her chair and fell at her husband's feet. The poor man was too feeble to move; all he could do was to force a pillow beneath her head with his feet. They were found the following morning, the man crying helplessly, his wife scarcely breathing. A doctor was summoned at once.

Diagnosis was simple; an empty bottle of sleeping capsules told the story eloquently. The patient was treated with intravenous injections of benzedrine every hour. The physician gauged her return to consciousness by administering a "lifeguard's injection"—by pushing his thumbnail against the tender skin beneath the patient's thumbnail. After a few hours this painful stimulus caused her to pull her hand away. In another few hours her face contorted with pain. Finally she stirred uneasily. By evening she could be roused by face slaps, and was out of danger, able to sleep off the effects of the drug. Some thirty-six more hours passed before she reached full consciousness.

Both her husband and her doctor then realized that her protestations required serious attention. She visited the latter after a few days and wept bitterly, demanding that she have something to do to fill the emptiness in her life. Talk made no impression; finally her doctor assured her that he would arrange some work for her at a hospital—but first she had to be examined physically, to insure her ability to withstand the arduous work.

The patient's eating habits had been abominable. She feared obesity, and ate but one meal a day, her dinner, after drinking coffee all day long. Such a diet almost guarantees hyperinsulinism. E.W. had it; she was treated for it. Her doctor, who never had any intention of finding her work, was never forced to refuse the request, for it was never made again. The patient recovered from her despondency (and hyperinsulinism); she became energetic and gay. She was able to help her husband through his serious illness, and their mutually better health has brought them complete happiness and understanding. And although there are sleeping potions in the home for her husband's use, E.W. never uses them.

A.F. is an artist in her early forties. Two years ago she was stricken with lobar pneumonia from which she recovered, thanks to penicillin. The increased load on her metabolic process, however, had extracted its toll. She began experiencing early-morning and late-afternoon weakness. Her eyes were also affected, and she was forced to give up a portrait commission she had been executing. She became terribly depressed. She was given the Glucose Tolerance Test and found to have hyperinsulinism. She was unable to follow the Harris diet, however, because she was living with a friend who ate and served a high carbohydrate diet. She became steadily worse.

[186]

Her husband had sustained severe financial losses. She had hoped to redress the balance with her work—but she could not work. Feeling useless and helpless, she no longer wanted to live. The thought of suicide became an obsession. She found and hid a bottle of sleeping medicine against the day when she could endure life no longer. Her husband became aware of the disappearance of the medicine and was frantic. At about this time they were at last able to move to their own apartment and so to go on the Harris diet. They seemed to have turned the corner but their financial difficulties continued. Her husband watched her for signs of improvement, always fearful that some crisis might detonate her urge to suicide. At last he found the hidden bottle for which he had been searching. He decided not to pour its contents down the drain but to test her death wish. Suddenly he thrust the bottle into her hand and told her to drink it down, believing that he had called her bluff. To his horror, she put it to her lips and, before he could knock it out of her hand, she had taken a good-sized swallow of it. It was not a lethal dose and all she got from it was her first good night's sleep in weeks. This proved to be the turning point. Gradually, but with increasing effectiveness, the diet and treatment took hold of her. Now, she is well on the way to complete recovery, all thought of suicide a thing of the past.

M.T., a man of forty-eight, had been brooding over domestic difficulties for many weeks. A few months ago he concluded that he could no longer go on living, and compulsively drank a bottle of tincture of iodine. He was rushed to a nearby hospital, from which he was transferred to the observation ward at Bellevue Hospital. His family asked Dr. Richard Hoffmann to treat the patient, and four days after the suicide attempt he was released in Dr. Hoffmann's custody. During the next two days he was given the Glucose Tolerance Test, which revealed a hyperinsulinism condition—the blood

[187]

glucose fell to 55 in five hours. The patient was placed on the Harris diet. Within a week he reported feeling much better, fully capable of accepting his role in life and completely aware of the folly of his compulsive act. Less than three weeks after the suicide attempt M.T. returned to work, feeling entirely fit. He has since faced and resolved his domestic problems realistically and sensibly.

Some of the more than eight thousand murders committed annually in the United States may also conceivably be due to hyperinsulinism. We refer not to the gang murders, or those for greed, but to those committed without any satisfactory motive. The murders that astonished Quentin Reynolds because they were committed by respectable people who had no prior police record—people who had never even received a ticket for a traffic violation. Almost every day one can read of murder committed by someone whom psychiatrists now unanimously declare insane, but who prior to the event had been considered perfectly sane. We know of only one such case in sufficient detail for discussion here, but it is typical of many.

In 1947 Anthony Papa lived quietly on Long Island, a good and kind man, respected by his community. He had never committed a crime, never "been in trouble." One day a neighbor made disparaging remarks about Tony Papa's wife. The remarks rankled Tony's pride. He feared that the slur might be repeated and thus injure his good reputation. He felt that he had to gain revenge from the neighbor, but he did not know how, and so he withdrew into himself and brooded about his lost prestige. Had he any real impulse for revenge, he managed to control it for some time.

One day, however, someone else taunted Tony about his wife, and the smoldering embers of revenge were rekindled. After brooding for some twenty-four hours without food or sleep, keeping himself alert with coffee, he decided to have it out with the neighbor. He went to the man's house, only to find him gone. For two hours Anthony Papa waited. Then suddenly, without warning, he brutally killed the neighbor's five-year-old daughter.

We do not intend to imply that Anthony Papa murdered because he had hyperinsulinism. We do not know enough about such complex urges, nor do we know enough about hyperinsulinism's relation to murder, to make such an assertion. Such speculation, moreover, is beside the point.

We do believe, however, that the chronic partial sugar starvation of his brain cells prepared Anthony Papa for his act by fogging his moral sense, distorting his normally realistic conception of his relationship to the world. It will be remembered that the brain waves of persons with low blood sugar are abnormal. It also will be remembered that a definite correlation has been established between low blood sugar, as part of a general metabolic imbalance, and certain types of insanity. We know that a twenty-four-hour diet of coffee (caffeine) was made to order for what subsequently evolved. It is hungry men who make revolutions, personal as well as social.

Insanity is not a medical but a legal term. A person legally is insane if he cannot distinguish between right and wrong and if he cannot understand the nature and quality of his acts. In many murder trials the defendant will plead insanity, in accordance with this legal definition. If he is found to be sane, his counsel may attempt to establish the defendant's insanity at the time of the crime. The prosecution invariably refutes such arguments and tries to prove in turn that the defendant is and was perfectly sane. Both defense and prosecution utilize the services of various psychiatrists to prove their respective cases.

Anthony Papa's attorney engaged Dr. Hoffmann, who had appeared in similar trials, to examine the defendant and to testify as to his findings.

Impressed by Anthony Papa's account of his day preceding the crime, Dr. Hoffmann requested permission to submit the accused to a six-hour Glucose Tolerance Test. I (Dr. Abrahamson) performed this test in the jail at Mineola, in the presence of the Nassau County medical examiner. The test indicated that Anthony Papa had hyperinsulinism!

Although they had little hope of convincing the jury of this discovery's significance, the medical experts did their best to explain it in court, in the hope of pointing out that there was at least a reasonable doubt of Papa's complete sanity at the time of the commission of the crime. It was impossible, however, to present such highly technical information convincingly. The jury decided that Anthony Papa was guilty of first degree murder, and he was sentenced to die in the electric chair.

Shortly before the completion of this book, the lay member of this collaboration became acquainted with "Narcotics Anonymous," an organization patterned after A.A. and concerned with the rehabilitation of the narcotics addict. The writer met a few of the members and gradually became aware of a rather peculiar habit common to them: all carried hard candies to suck on. When asked about this, one N.A. member remarked that "it seems to make it easier to do without the stuff."

On another occasion the lay member attended an open meeting of N.A. A young man who had been an addict for only two years was telling his story—how he had become a marijuana smoker and, after a while, having been told that "reefers" were sissy stuff, had taken up heroin.

"Of course," observed the chairman of the meeting, "it wouldn't have happened if he hadn't been neurotic to begin with. All of us are a bit neurotic or we wouldn't become addicts."

These two facts had a familiar ring. A craving for the solace of sugar and the neuroses were old friends of ours by now. Could it be that hyperinsulinism had something to do with addiction? The pieces fell into place: morphine has an action similar to that of caffeine in causing a sudden rise in blood sugar. The withdrawal symptoms of morphine—visceral colics, cold sweats, muscular and vascular cramps, and collapse—are found in insulin shock.

Our next step was obvious. We must subject a few drug addicts to the six-hour Glucose Tolerance Test.

A highly intelligent and talented man of forty, L.M. has been using morphine for at least fifteen years. Recently he "took a cure." Physical examination revealed the left upper abdominal tenderness and spasm associated with hyperinsulinism. When given the Glucose Tolerance Test, L.M.'s blood sugar fell from 92 to 58 mg. of glucose per 100 cc. in five hours. L.M. said he felt as if he "could use a shot." After breakfast the urge *apparently* was relieved.

A.B. is an underprivileged, poorly educated boy of eighteen who was promoted to heroin from reefers during the past two years. He voluntarily took the cure at the U. S. Government Hospital at Lexington, Kentucky. During A.B.'s Glucose Tolerance Test, his sugar tolerance curve followed a similar pattern, starting at 86 and dropping to 62 in six hours.

Both patients were started on the hyperinsulinism diet. Neither would cooperate, however, refusing to follow the diet and constantly missing appointments for calcium injections.

We soon realized that proper investigation and treatment of this phenomenon is utterly impossible unless the patients are under rigid control. We therefore are respectfully referring this problem to those government agencies having the patients and the means for such study.

Among the signs and symptoms behind which hyperinsulinism masquerades, Seale Harris included those of *petit mal* (mild epilepsy). It is significant, therefore, that some women who suffered from epilepsy appeared to improve during pregnancy, as rheumatoid arthritis and peptic ulcer patients did—when the blood glucose tends to be higher. Other pregnant epileptics, however, seemed to suffer more severely.[1] A number of persons subject to epileptic seizures were given the Glucose Tolerance Test, which indicated low sugar tolerance curves.[2] It also has been found that the brain wave tracings of persons afflicted with petit mal were similar to those of hyperinsulinism victims.[3] While these facts are insufficient in themselves to indicate that epilepsy is a manifestation of hyperinsulinism, they provide enough evidence to warrant further investigation of the relationship between the two diseases.

Less than two years ago, Dr. John A. Schindler, chief physician of the Monroe, Wisconsin, Clinic, delivered an address over the University of Wisconsin's radio station, WHA. His remarks were published in the *Reader's Digest* (December, 1949) and released to a shocked world.

"Fifty per cent of all the people going to doctors in the United States today are victims of this one disease," Dr. Schindler stated. "Many would put the figure higher. At the Ochsner Clinic in New Orleans a report was published reviewing 500 consecutive admissions to that institution; of those, 386 or 77 per cent were sick with this one disease."

What *is* this disease?

"It used to be called psychoneurosis," Dr. Schindler went on. "Now it is known as psychosomatic illness. And it is *not* a disease in which the patient just *thinks* he is sick. The pain is often just as severe as the pain from a gall-bladder colic.

"Psychosomatic illness isn't produced by a bacterium, or by a virus, or by a new growth. It is produced by the circumstances of daily living. I have tried to find one word for it, but it takes three, each of them meaning about the same thing but in different degrees. They are: *cares, difficulties, troubles.* Whenever one has such a thick, inpenetrable layer of c.d.t. that he can't get up above it into a realm of joy and pleasure occasionally, he gets a psychosomatic illness."

Cares, difficulties, and troubles are not far from Dr. Portis' life situations which caused emotions to be relayed through the hypothalamus via the vagi to the islets of the pancreas, causing an oversecretion of insulin with consequent lowering of the blood sugar level. We realize, of course, that Dr. Schindler spoke before Dr. Portis had reported fully on his findings and only a very short time after the medical member of this collaboration and Dr. Hoffmann had reported on theirs. For this very reason, however—his apparent unawareness of the interrelationship of hyperinsulinism and the neuroses, and of the mechanism whereby life situations may contribute to setting up the vicious circle of hyperinsulinism—Dr. Schindler's description of the symptoms of what is now called psychosomatic disease becomes all the more significant.

Dr. Schindler described the various parts of the body that are the first to reveal tension as a result of psychosomatic disease—the muscles at the back of the neck and at the upper end of the esophagus. Then he tells us, "much more commonly the stomach is involved." He describes the pain as being "just as bad as an ulcer. In our town we had a grocer who had a pain exactly like that of an ulcer. He had plenty of trouble—a competitive business, a nagging wife, a wayward son—and he had the pain most of the time. Doctors assured him he had no ulcer. He finally began to believe them when he noticed that every time he went fishing the pain disappeared. And it didn't come back until he was almost home."

It will be remembered that persons with a real peptic ulcer as well as those who had no visible ulcer were both found to have hyperinsulinism. Dr. Schindler went on to say that the pain might occur "lower down in the colon," and when it did, it would "seem just like appendicitis." Seale Harris listed appendicitis as one of the conditions under which hyperinsulinism masquerades. Among many other symptoms described by Dr. Schindler is the pain in the left upper portion of the chest to which we also have made previous reference. He also refers briefly to "the effect that the emotion has on the endocrine system."

While the usual therapy for the so-called psychosomatic diseases is sometimes effective, we believe that the steadily increasing incidence of these ailments is patent proof of the insufficiency of such treatment. We refuse to believe that Americans are becoming a people who "can't take it." We prefer to believe that they are a people who have been beguiled by a good deal of high pressure advertising into bad dietary habits and by an incredible lot of nonsense posing as science into bad living and thinking habits. Admittedly they are also living through one of the greatest crises that has ever confronted the human race. It is a crisis that impinges upon them at every angle of their individual and social lives. It creates a plethora of emotion-arousing life situations. What is needed is an understanding of their true nature and, for the individual who succumbs to them and to his bad habits and contracts this convenient psychosomatic disease, we humbly suggest a little more emphasis upon the *soma* and a little less on the overworked *psyche*.

Specifically, we recommend to doctors and laymen alike in dealing with the psychosomatic, a thorough physical check-up, *including the sugar tolerance test*. It is high time that we realized that *blood sugar* is as important as an indication of health or disease as blood pressure or blood temperature.

And should any of these psychosomatics prove to have the low blood sugar of hyperinsulinism, we respectfully suggest placing them on the proper diet to arrest it. Then whatever psychotherapy is needed will be administered more easily. They will begin to look upon the bright side of life for adult reasons and without undergoing the therapeutic bathos of a cult of false and childish optimism, which our great nation is happily outgrowing.

What have we been trying to say in this book? We have been trying to call attention to a condition that needs correcting. The only reasonable authority on this earth is that of scientifically determined truths—truths upon whose secure foundations we can build things that work in useful ways.

There is no greater evil on earth than ignorance of such truths when they are available. That a condition, as far-reaching as hyperinsulinism seems to be, should have been so long the stepchild of medicine is glaring evidence of the subtle retrogression of civilization in the past quarter century of bewilderment and vain search for short cuts and panaceas in every field.

We do not say that all that we have written here is true. We do say that we would not have written it unless we had *believed* it true. It seems to us that the evidence we have presented points to the truth sufficiently to challenge others better equipped to investigate further into the facts we have rescued from the dark closet of professional and lay indifference.

We believe that in 1924 Seale Harris discovered a golden key that will unlock many tightly closed doors. We have indicated some of them. There may be others. Let us try the key in those many locks and see if the doors will open.

Notes

NOTE I, p. 21

THE CHEMIST writes the formula for formic acid: H.COOH.

The COOH group is known as carboxyl, the acid group: It is composed of an atom each of carbon and hydrogen and two of oxygen.

Acetic acid, $CH_3.COOH$, is next in the series. The hydrogen has been replaced by CH_3, the methyl group. The rest of the series have longer groups of carbon and hydrogen atoms. Thus, proprionic acid, the third member of the family, is $CH_3.CH_2.COOH$.

As the series continues, the number of CH_2 groups in the line increases. Hence, the fourth is butyric acid: $CH_3.CH_2.-CH_2.COOH$. In combination with glycerin, butyric acid is butter fat.

Eventually the series reaches stearic acid, which is found in tallow. Its chemical formula contains sixteen CH_2 groups.

There are, of course, other fatty acids in our foods. Some of them do not consist of groups strung out in a single chain; they have side groups, like a lavaliere hanging from a necklace. In others there is a deficiency in hydrogen. For our purposes, however, our attention is confined to the straight-chained, saturated fatty acids.

[196]

An added note of interest: only those fatty acids with an even number of carbon atoms in their chains occur in our foods.

NOTE II, p. 22

LET US consider the step-wise process of the burning of fats, taking stearic acid as an example. Its structural formula is:

$$CH_3.CH_2.CH_2.CH_2.CH_2.CH_2.CH_2.CH_2.CH_2.CH_2.CH_2.CH_2.-$$
$$CH_2.CH_2.CH_2.CH_2.CH_2.COOH.$$

In the body the second, or beta, carbon atom (atoms are labeled according to the Greek alphabet from the carboxyl group) undergoes oxidation and is changed into CHOH. Oxidation then consumes the two hydrogen atoms of the new group, burning them to water (H_2O) and leaving CO, which is called the ketone group. The steps of the process are:

$$CH_3.CH_2.CH_2.CH_2.CH_2.CH_2.CH_2.CH_2.CH_2.CH_2.CH_2.CH_2.-$$
$$CH_2.CH_2.CH_2.CHOH.CH_2.COOH,$$

and

$$CH_3.CH_2.CH_2.CH_2.CH_2.CH_2.CH_2.CH_2.CH_2.CH_2.CH_2.CH_2.-$$
$$CH_2.CH_2.CH_2.CO.CH_2.COOH.$$

The last three carbon groups are readily oxidized, the CO becoming COOH (the acid group) and the other two combining with oxygen to form CO_2 and H_2O (carbonic acid and water). This leaves:

$$CH_3.CH_2.CH_2.CH_2.CH_2.CH_2.CH_2.CH_2.CH_2.CH_2.CH_2.CH_2.-$$
$$CH_2.CH_2.CH_2.COOH,$$

which is an acid with two less carbon atoms.

This process continues, the carbon chain becoming shorter by two carbon atoms with each step. Finally we reach:

$$CH_3.CH_2.CH_2.COOH \text{ (butyric acid).}$$

The same process of oxidation of the beta carbon atom yields:

$$CH_3.CHOH.CH_2.COOH \text{ (beta oxybutyric acid),}$$

and then:

$$CH_3.CO.CH_2.COOH \text{ (diacetic acid).}$$

This should in turn split off two carbon atoms like its predecessors, and normally it does so, forming:

$$CH_3.COOH \text{ (acetic acid),}$$

which is readily oxidized.

Thus the fat is completely burned into carbonic acid gas and water.

When carbohydrate is not burned completely, as in diabetes and also as in starvation, the last step in the burning of fat does not take place. It is not known why this interruption occurs.

NOTE III, p. 22

CHEMICALLY this may be expressed:

$$CH_3.CO.CH_2.COOH \longrightarrow CO_2 + CH_3.CO.CH_3.$$

References

CHAPTER 2

1. R. H. Major, ed., *Classic Descriptions of Disease* (Springfield, Ill., Thomas, 1932), p. 186.
2. *Ibid.*, pp. 191–194.
3. *Ibid.*, pp. 186–188.
4. J. Von Mering and O. Minkowski, *Arch. exper. Path. Pharm.*, 26; 371, 1889.
5. P. Langerhans, *Beitrage zur mikroschopischen Anatomie der Bauchspeichedruse* (Berlin, 1869).
6. E. L. Opie, *Bull. Johns Hopkins Hosp.*, 12; 263, 1901.
7. F. G. Banting and C. H. Best, *J. Lab. clin. Med.*, 7; 265, 1922.
8. K. B. Turner and E. H. Bidwell, *J. Exp. Med.*, 62; 721, 1917.
9. J. W. Gofman, F. Lindgren, H. Elliott, W. Mantz, J. Hewitt, B. Strisouer, V. Herring, and T. P. Lyon, *Science, N.S. 111;* 166, 1950.
10. D. Adlersberg and O. Porges, *Klin. Woch.*, 6; 2371, 1927.
11. H. P. Himsworth and E. M. Marshall, *Clinical Science*, 2; 95, 1935.
12. Himsworth, *Clinical Science*, 2; 117, 1935.
13. J. J. Abel, E. M. K. Geiling, C. A. Rouiller, F. K. Bell, and O. Wintersteiner, *J. Pharm. Exp. Ther.*, 31; 65, 1927.

14. H. C. Hagedorn, B. N. Jensen, N. B. Krarup, and I. J. Wodstrup, *J.A.M.A.*, *106;* 177, 1936.
15. L. Reiner, D. S. Searle, and E. H. Lang, *J. Pharm. Exp. Ther.*, *67;* 330, 1939.
16. F. Bischoff, *Am. J. Physiol.*, *117;* 182, 1936.
17. F. B. Peck, *Proc. Am. Diab. Assoc.*, *2;* 69, 1942.
18. C. Krayenbühl and T. Rosenberg, *Rep. Steno Mem. Hosp.*, *1;* 60, 1946.
19. C. Bernard, *Compt. rend. soc. biol.*, *1;* 60, 1850.
20. B. A. Houssay, V. G. Foglia, F. S. Smyth, C. T. Rietti, and A. B. Houssay, *J. Exp. Med.*, *75;* 547, 1942.
21. R. E. Haist, J. Campbell, and C. H. Best, *New England J. Med.*, *223;* 607, 1940.
22. Von Mering, *Verhan. Kong. inn. Med.*, *5;* 185, 1886.
23. J. S. Dunn, H. L. Sheehan, and N. G. B. McLetchie, *Lancet, 1;* 484, 1943.
24. H. J. John, *Endocrinology, 18;* 75, 1934.
25. W. G. Exton and A. R. Rose, *Am. J. Clin. Path., 4;* 381, 1934.
26. L. Hamman and I. I. Hirschman, *Arch. Internal Med., 20;* 761, 1917.
27. H. Gray, *Arch. Internal Med., 31;* 241, 259, 1923.

CHAPTER 3

1. S. Harris, *J.A.M.A., 83;* 729, 1924.
2. Harris, *Ann. Internal Med., 10;* 514, 1936.
3. S. H. Gray and L. C. Femmster, *Arch. Path. Lab. Med., 1;* 348, 1926.
4. R. M. Wilder, F. N. Allan, M. H. Power, and H. E. Robertson, *J.A.M.A., 89;* 348, 1927.
5. W. R. Campbell, R. R. Graham, and W. L. Robinson, *Am. J. Med. Sci., 198;* 445, 1939.
6. A. O. Whipple and V. K. Frantz, *Ann. Surgery, 101;* 1299, 1935.

7. Harris, *The Mississippi Doctor, 13;* 9, 1936.
8. J. W. Conn and E. S. Conn, *Arch. Internal Med., 68;* 876, 1941.

CHAPTER 4

1. Leonardo Botallo, *Opera Omnia* (Leyden, 1660), p. 20.
2. F. A. Simon, *Specialities in Medical Practice* (New York, Nelson, n.d.), p. 303.
3. *Ibid.,* p. 308.
4. *Ibid.,* p. 303.
5. *Ibid.,* p. 312.
6. W. T. Vaughan, *Strange Malady* (Garden City Publishing Company, 1943).
7. A. Q. Maisel, "Allergies," *McCall's* (September, 1950).
8. A. Myerson, *Speaking of Man* (New York, Knopf, 1950).
9. Maisel, *op. cit.*
10. J. H. Black, *Texas State Med. J.,* 39; 257, 1933.
    E. P. Joslin, *The Treatment of Diabetes Mellitus* (4th ed.; Philadelphia, Lea and Febiger, 1928), p. 733.
    H. B. Wilmer, M. M. Miller, and J. T. Beardwood, *Southern Med. J.,* 29; 197, 1936.
    J. T. Malone, *U.S. Veterans' Bur. Med. Bull.,* 5; 285, 1929.
    G. L. Waldbott, M. S. Ascher, and S. Rosenzweig, *J. Allergy, 10;* 220, 1939.
11. R. A. Kern, *Trans. Am. Assoc. Phys.,* 49; 23, 1934.
12. Joslin, *The Treatment of Diabetes Mellitus* (6th ed.; 1939), p. 446.
    Joslin, H. F. Root, P. White, and A. Marble, *The Treatment of Diabetes Mellitus* (7th ed.; 1940), p. 414.
    N. Swern, *J. Allergy,* 2; 375, 1931.
    Joslin, *The Treatment of Diabetes Mellitus,* 4th ed., p. 734.
13. L. Levi and H. de Rothschild, *La Petite insuffisance thyroidenne et son traitment* (1913), p. 80.

14. H. A. Rusk, T. E. Weichselbaum, and M. Somogyi, *J.A.M.A.*, *142*; 2395, 1930.
15. H. R. Sandstead and A. J. Beams, *Arch. Internal Med.*, *61*; 371, 1938.
16. S. Harris, *Ann. Internal Med.*, *10*; 514, 1936.
17. E. M. Abrahamson, *J. Clin. Endocrinol.*, *1*; 402, 1941. .
18. J. F. Goodhart, *Albutt's System of Medicine*, 5; 287, 1899.
19. H. W. Barber and G. H. Oriel, *Lancet*, 2; 1009, 1928.
    A. V. Stoesser, *J. Allergy*, 3; 332, 1932.
    A. V. Stoesser and M. M. Cook, *Lancet*, *58*; 12, 1938.
20. A. Prince, *N.Y. State Med. J.*, *40*; 1385, 1940.
21. M. M. Peskin and A. H. Fineman, *Am. J. Dis. Child.*, *39*; 1240, 1930.
22. E. L. Ross, *J. Biol. Chem.*, *34*; 335, 1918.
23. F. P. Underhill and D. H. Sprunt, *Proc. Soc. Exp. Biol. Med.*, *25*; 137, 1927.
24. L. Pollack and W. Robitschek, *Wien. klin. Woch.*, *39*; 753, 1926.
25. R. S. Lyman, E. Nichols, and W. S. McCann, *J. Pharm. Exp. Ther.*, *21*; 343, 1924.
26. E. M. Abrahamson, *U.S. Naval Med. Bull.*, *40*; 711, 1942.
27. *Ibid.*
28. S. A. Levine, *Clinical Heart Disease* (1st ed.; Philadelphia, Saunders, 1926), p. 24.
29. Joslin, *The Treatment of Diabetes Mellitus*, 4th ed., p. 712.
30. Abrahamson, *J. Clin. Endocrinol.*, *4*; 71, 1944.
31. A. F. Coburn and L. V. Moore, *Am. J. Dis. Child.*, *65*; 744, 1943.
32. E. C. Warner, F. G. Winterton, and M. L. Clark, *Quart. J. Med.*, *4*; 227, 1935.
33. M. P. Schultz, *J.A.M.A.*, *111*; 1961, 1938.
34. D. Adlersberg and O. Porges, *Klin. Woch.*, *6*; 2371, 1927.

35. R. E. Rothenberg and L. Teicher, *Am. J. Digestive Diseases*, 5; 663, 1938.

36. Joslin, Root, White, and Marble, *The Treatment of Diabetes Mellitus*, 7th ed., p. 468.

37. Hinsworth and Marshall, *Clinical Science*, 2; 95, 1935. Hinsworth, *Clinical Science*, 2; 117, 1935.

38. C. R. Stockard, *Medicine*, 5; 116, 1926.

39. Harris, *Am. J. Digestive Diseases*, 2; 557, 1935.

40. J. P. Quigley, V. Johnson, and E. I. Solomon, *Am. J. Physiol.*, 90; 89, 1929.

41. Abrahamson, *Am. J. Digestive Diseases*, 12; 379, 1945.

CHAPTER 5

1. S. Harris, *Ann. Internal Med.*, 10; 514, 1936. Harris, *J.A.M.A.*, 83; 729, 1924.

2. C. L. Derrick, *Oxford Looseleaf Medicine*, IV, 178 (28).

3. E. M. Abrahamson, *Bull. Reg. Med. Tech.*, 1; 138, 1940.

4. R. H. Hoffmann and Abrahamson, *Am. J. Digestive Diseases*, 16; 242, 1949.

5. M. Fabrykant and B. L. Pacella, *Proc. Am. Diabetic Assoc.*, 7; 233, 1947.

6. E. H. Parsons, E. Ronzoni-Bishop, S. Hulbert, and E. F. Gildea, *Science News Letter*, 53; 342, 1948.

7. A. T. Cameron, *Recent Advances in Endocrinology* (2d ed.; Philadelphia, Blakiston, 1934), p. 162.

8. Harris, *Ann. Internal Med.*, 10; 514, 1936. Harris, *J.A.M.A.*, 83; 729, 1924.

9. T. A. C. Rennie and J. E. Howard, *Psychosom. Med.*, 4; 273, 1936.

10. S. A. Portis and I. H. Zitman, *J.A.M.A.*, 121; 569, 1943.

11. Portis and F. Alexander, *Psychosom. Med.*, 6; 191, 1944 Portis, *J.A.M.A.*, 126; 413, 1944; 142; 1281, 1950.

Portis, Zitman, and C. H. Lawrence, *J.A.M.A.*, *144;* 1162, 1950.

12. Portis, personal communication to A. W. P., August 3, 1950.
13. W. C. Alvarez, *Ill. Med. J.*, *83;* 4, 1943.
14. *Ibid.*
15. F. Sondern, Jr., *Reader's Digest* (May, 1950), p. 73.
16. *Ibid.*
17. *Ibid.*
18. E. F. Lutz, *Ind. Med.*, 2; 599, 1946.
19. S. C. Franco, *Ind. Med.*, *19;* 213, 1950.
20. Portis, *J.A.M.A.*, *126;* 413, 1944; *142;* 1281, 1950.
21. Alvarez, *Ill. Med. J.*, *83;* 4, 1943.
22. Portis, Zitman, and Lawrence, *J.A.M.A.*, *144;* 1162, 1950.
23. *Ibid.*

CHAPTER 6

1. C. L. Walker, *Harper's Magazine* (July, 1950), p. 29.
2. M. Mann, *Primer on Alcoholism* (New York, Rinehart and Company, 1950), pp. vii, 72.
3. C. C. Furnas, *The Next 100 Years* (Baltimore, Williams and Wilkins, 1938), pp. 156–157.
4. L. Hogben, *Science for the Citizen* (Garden City Publishing Company, 1943), p. 495.
5. H. Reilly, *Easy Does It* (New York, P. J. Kenedy and Sons, 1950), p. 191.
6. C. H. Durfee, paper read at a meeting of the A.A.A.S., December, 1938.
7. Durfee, *J. Crim. Psychopath.*, 3; 278, 1941.
8. Durfee, *Quart. J. Stud. Alc.*, 7; 229, 1946.
9. Durfee, *Rhode Island Med. J.*, *30;* 651, 1938.
10. *Ibid.*, p. 692.
11. W. B. Farbstein, *Fate*, *4;* 3, 1950.
12. Reilly, *op. cit.*, p. 275.

13. W. L. Laurence, *Look* (July 18, 1950), p. 53.
    H. W. Lovell, *Hope and Help for the Alcoholic* (New York, Doubleday, 1951), p. 15.

CHAPTER 7

1. G. H. Scott, *Biological Symposia, 10;* 277, 1943.
2. D. W. Bronk, *Science in Progress, Fourth Series,* ed. George Baitsell (New Haven, Yale University Press, 1945), p. 49.
3. M. Fabrykant and B. L. Pacella, *Proc. Am. Diabetic Assoc., 7;* 233, 1947.
4. R. H. Hoffmann and E. M. Abrahamson, *Am. J. Digestive Diseases, 16;* 242, 1949.
5. B. A. Houssay, V. G. Foglia, F. S. Smyth, C. T. Rietti, and A. B. Houssay, *J. Exp. Med., 75;* 547, 1942.
6. F. G. Young, *Lancet, 2;* 372, 1937.
7. C. H. Best and N. B. Taylor, *The Physiological Basis of Medical Practice* (3d ed.; Baltimore, Williams and Wilkins, 1943), p. 1160.
8. W. R. Hess, *Schweiz. Arch. Neurol. Psychiat., 16;* 36, 1925.
9. W. W. Swingle and J. J. Pfiffner, *Medicine, 11;* 371, 1932.
10. E. C. Kendall, *Trans. New York Acad. Sci., 50;* 540, 1949.
11. C. N. H. Long and F. D. W. Lukens, *J. Exp. Med., 63;* 465, 1936.
12. F. D. W. Lukens and F. C. Dohan, *Endocrinology, 30;* 175, 1942.
13. D. J. Ingle, *Endocrinology, 29;* 649, 1941.
14. T. Reichstein and C. W. Shoppee, in *Vitamins and Hormones,* eds. R. S. Harris and K. V. Thimann (New York, Academic Press, 1943), I, 345.
15. Kendall, *Trans. New York Acad. Sci., 50;* 540, 1949.
16. L. H. Sarett, *J. Am. Chem. Soc., 70;* 1454, 1948.
17. Kendall, *Ann. Internal Med., 37;* 791, 1950.

18. *Ibid.*

19. P. S. Hench, *Proc. Staff Meet. Mayo Clin., 13;* 161, 1938.

20. L. Granirer, lecture to the Society for Medical Jurisprudence, November 13, 1950.

21. Hench, C. H. Slocumb, E. C. Kendall, and H. F. Polley, *Proc. Staff Meet. Mayo Clin., 24;* 181, 1949.

22. Hench, Slocumb, Kendall, Polley, A. R. Barnes, and H. L. Smith, *Proc. Staff Meet. Mayo Clin., 24;* 277, 1949.

23. D. Adlersberg, L. Schaeffer, and S. R. Drachman, *J.A.M.A., 144;* 909, 1950.

24. J. E. Howard and R. A. Carey, *J. Clin. Endocrinol., 9;* 691, 1949.

25. B. Rose, J. A. P. Pare, K. Pump, and R. L. Stanfford, *Can. Med. Assoc. J., 62;* 6, 1950.

26. Hench, *Proc. Staff Meet. Mayo Clin., 24;* 167, 1949.

27. D. J. Sandweiss, H. C. Saltzstein, S. R. Scheinberg, and A. Parks, *J.A.M.A., 144;* 1436, 1950.

28. Personal communication.

29. Abrahamson, *Am. J. Dig. Dis.,* on press.

30. W. Q. Wolfson and C. Cohn, *Proc. of the First Clinical ACTH Conference,* ed. by J. R. Mote (Philadelphia, Blakiston, 1950), p. 241.

31. Joslin, Root, White, and Marble, *The Treatment of Diabetes Mellitus,* 7th ed., p. 87.

CHAPTER 8

1. S. A. Kinnier Wilson, *Neurology,* ed. A. Ninian Bruce (Baltimore, Williams and Wilkins, 1941), p. 1526.

2. G. W. J. Mackay and H. Barbash, *J. Mental Sci., 77;* 83, 1931.

3. M. Fabrykant and B. L. Pacella, *Proc. Am. Diabetic Assoc., 7;* 234, 1947.

CPSIA information can be obtained
at www.ICGtesting.com
Printed in the USA
LVOW04s0546191115

463283LV00017B/234/P